BLASPHEMY
Ancient & Modern

NICOLAS WALTER

RATIONALIST PRESS
ASSOCIATION

London, 1990

Blasphemy Ancient & Modern

First published in February 1990

© Rationalist Press Association 1990

ISBN 0 301 90001 9

Published by the Rationalist Press Association
(with the Committee Against Blasphemy Law)
88 Islington High Street
London N1 8EW
England

Printed by RAP Ltd.
201 Spotland Road
Rochdale OL12 7AF
England

Contents

Dedication

A toast written by W. J. Fox and used from 1817 at the celebrations of the organisation which later became the South Place Ethical Society:

To the cause of civil and religious liberty, all over the world.

A toast written by Edward Clodd and used from 1919 at the celebrations of the Rationalist Press Association:

To the immortal memory of the men and women through whose courage and suffering we have entered the kingdom of the free.

Illustrations

Front cover

'Nuptials of God' by Eric Gill, from the *Game* (January 1923) — see page 68.

Back cover

'Moses Getting a Back View' from the *Freethinker* (December 1882) — see page 52. ·

Preface

Blasphemy Ancient & Modern is intended not as an academic study of the history of blasphemy or as a technical account of the laws against blasphemy, but as a critical view of the subject from the point of view of the blasphemers rather than of the religions they offended or the laws they transgressed. It is written in the belief that freedom of expression in religious as in other controversial matters is a precious possession, and in the hope that the story it tells will be both interesting and instructive.

Thomas Paine wrote at the beginning of his third *Crisis* paper in 1777:

We are not only apt to forget the ground we have travelled over, but frequently neglect to gather up experience as we go.... As it is pleasant and sometimes useful to look back ... and trace the turns and windings through which we have passed, so we may likewise derive many advantages by halting a while ... and taking a review of the wondrous labyrinth of little more than yesterday.

He also wrote at the beginning of his fourth *Crisis* paper in 1777: 'Those who expect to reap the blessings of freedom must ... undergo the fatigues of supporting it.' What is needed in the area of freedom of expression about religion is informed knowledge and determined action.

The history of Freethought is to a large extent the history of attempts to prevent it. The Freethought movement in Britain developed over a long period partly through a series of battles against both Church and State in which one of the main weapons was the blasphemy law and one of the commonest battlegrounds the resulting court cases. In this war there was from time to time a pause, during which the law seemed to have fallen into disuse and was forgotten; but after a time it was revived, the cases resumed, and the war continued. The latest pause lasted for more than half a century, from the 1920s to the 1970s, until the law was revived once more by the *Gay News* case.

Since then the law and practice of blasphemy have been the subject of much discussion, especially when other potential cases have arisen, but most of the contributions to the discussion have been more or less badly informed and badly argued. *Blasphemy Ancient & Modern* is an attempt to bring light into an obscure place, by putting blasphemy into its ideological and historical context, describing the past experience and discussing the present situation with some care and in some detail, and ending with a plea for the end of this relic of religious persecution.

The coverage is confined mainly to Britain, not because of lack of interest in or awareness of other countries, but because of lack of knowledge of and space for their experiences. Similar accounts could be written of similar events outside Britain, and this particular attempt should be considered as only a single contribution to the documentation of religious persecution around the world. The coverage is confined entirely to religion, not because of lack of interest in or awareness of other forms of persecution, but because of the wish to emphasise the important point that most ideological persecution has derived from religious intolerance.

★   ★   ★

During the late 1970s the *New Humanist* (the journal of the Rationalist Press Association, one of the main organisations in the British Freethought movement) published several articles on the various aspects and stages of the *Gay News* case. One of these articles — a long account of the history of the law and the trial of *Gay News* (May/August 1977) — was quickly written and quickly reprinted as a pamphlet — *Blasphemy In Britain* (1977) — which immediately went out of print and out of date. *Blasphemy Ancient & Modern* incorporates a revision of that publication, taking into account the other articles and adding a great deal of new material.

Thanks are due to the many previous workers in this field, to the libraries and publications where the research was done and the material was found, to the friends and colleagues who gave suggestions or made comments at various times, to the audiences at various meetings who contributed further ideas, to the experts who corrected errors, and especially to Jim Herrick, William McIlroy, Terry Mullins, Barbara Smoker, and Christine Walter.

Nicolas Walter   January 1990

1 Introduction

Blasphemy is one among many forms of expression which are considered to be objectionable. Every society, indeed every human group (if not every human individual), objects to some forms of expression for one reason or another; and every society imposes on such forms of expression limits of one kind or another — whether the informal ones of custom and taste (enforced by the community through public opinion), or the formal ones of the law (enforced by the authorities through the courts).

In our society, the various forms of objectionable expression which are treated as illegal may be conveniently classified according to category and intensity as follows:

Political   *Treason* for extreme material, *sedition* for serious material, and lesser offences such as revealing official secrets or incitement to disaffection.

Personal   *Defamation*, whether written (*libel*) or spoken (*slander*).

Social   A relatively new category, covering such things as *racism* (and possibly *sexism* in the near future) which fall between political and personal offence.

Sexual   *Obscenity* for extreme material, *indecency* for mild material.

Religious   *Heresy* for serious material, *profanity* for trivial material, and *blasphemy* for material in between.

These forms of expression are generally dealt with by the authorities through the criminal law, on the understanding that they do not just offend the feelings of particular individuals but threaten the stability of the general community ('the peace'). The one exception is that personal defamation is generally dealt with by the offended person through the civil law — though there is also the law of criminal libel covering serious defamation which might have serious public consequences. Objectionable forms of expression about religion have usually been considered as crimes against both Church and State, and have frequently been treated as serious offences.

★   ★   ★

Aristotle said at the beginning of the *Politics* that the clearest view of a subject is obtained by considering its origin and development; this is certainly true of blasphemy. The practice and punishment of blasphemy — and of heresy and profanity — belong to the long and wide tradition of religious dissent and persecution. The epic history of this tradition is beyond our scope here, but it must be taken as the background to the present discussion. The legal historian Frederick Pollock suggested that religious persecution passed through four chronological stages — tribal, theological, political, and social — depending on whether religious dissent was believed to endanger the kin group, the Church, the State, or society ('The Theory of Persecution', *Essays on Jurisprudence and Ethics*, 1882). The truth seems to be rather that the four forms overlap, and that religious unorthodoxy has been attacked at different times or the same time for endangering any or all of the four entities.

Blasphemy (from the Greek *blasphēmia*, meaning offensive speech, especially in religious matters) may be defined very broadly as any offensive expression concerning God or the gods, other sacred persons or objects, religious doctrines or ideas, scriptures or liturgies, institutions or practices. It has generally been taken less seriously than the deliberate rejection of the doctrines of the prevailing religion (heresy) and more seriously than casual rudeness about religious matters (profanity). Sometimes it is punished very severely indeed, to the extent of torture and death, and sometimes it isn't punished at all. A typical contradiction may be found in the Roman Empire. The Emperor Tiberius was reported by Tacitus (in his *Annals*) to have remarked in the first century AD that 'offences to the gods are the affairs of the gods' ('*deorum injurias dis curae*'); but Roman citizens had to pay their respects and make their sacrifices to the deified Emperor himself on pain of death.

Even otherwise very tolerant societies have persecuted religious dissent. Ancient Athens, which is famous for being one of the main sources of European culture and civilisation, is also infamous for putting Socrates to death in 399 BC because of his unorthodox ideas about religion. And he was far from being the only victim of religious orthodoxy there. The philosopher Anaxagoras and the sculptor Phidias were imprisoned, the philosophers Protagoras and

Aristotle were driven into exile, Pericles's companion the hostess Aspasia and the dramatist Euripides were prosecuted. Yet Homer and Aristophanes were not only allowed to mock the gods in their poems and plays but were honoured for it. Indeed Plato, the greatest pupil of Socrates, considered the well-known accounts of the pagan deities in Greek mythology and literature to be so blasphemous that they should be banned in the ideal state described in his *Republic*; and he proposed a full-scale religious inquisition and the death penalty for impiety in the even more authoritarian state described in his *Laws*.

One reason why these events and ideas are known is that Athens was a relatively open society in which such things were recorded and discussed. Far fewer cases are known in closed societies where persecution is very much worse, and it may be assumed that blasphemy is a virtually universal offence. Indeed it seems that in most places and at most times any open challenge to prevailing religious beliefs has been suppressed by force. In particular, all established religions which have possessed political power have persecuted blasphemy, and none more so than the powerful monotheistic religions of Judaism, Christianity and Islam. Blasphemy has always been considered to threaten religion, and it especially threatens the concentrated monopoly of monotheistic religion, with its single all-powerful, all-knowing, all-good, all-loving but all-angry god. The practice and punishment of blasphemy must be seen in this ideological and historical context.

The laws enforcing religious persecution must also be seen in a practical context. Even when they are not overtly used — and prosecutions for plasphemy and profanity have indeed been rare for well over half a century — they are still covertly used to limit free expression in the area of religion, since their continued existence allows the official authorities and the unofficial vigilantists to exert a form of pressure through threats and warnings which would not be tolerated in any other controversial area. The law of blasphemy is still far from obsolete, and its theory and history therefore remain regrettably relevant topics.

2 Religion & Blasphemy

Blasphemy is an essential element of the Judaeo-Christian religion, because of the very nature of that religion. Jewish monotheism developed not only as a constructive affirmation of a Jewish tribal god but also as a destructive negation of non-Jewish tribal gods, and it displayed great sensitivity both about dissent from its own particular deity and about assent to any rival deity. Indeed the Jewish god was seen as being so sacred that it was blasphemous not only to deny his uniqueness or insult his nature but even to say or write his name (Yahweh or Jehovah).

Any such offence — along with a great many others — was theoretically punished by death in the Law attributed to Moses in the first books of the Bible and asserted as the basis of Judaism. In one curious passage God commands: 'Thou shalt not revile the gods [sic]' (*Exodus* xxii, 28). In another passage God specifically makes blasphemy a capital offence: 'He that blasphemeth the name of the Lord, he shall surely be put to death, and all the congregation shall surely stone him' (*Leviticus* xxiv, 16). It is impossible to know how far this was actually put into practice, but instances are recorded in both parts of the Bible (Naboth in 1 *Kings* xxi, and Stephen in *Acts* vi).

Yet Judaism — or indeed any form of moralistic monotheism — involves the theoretical impossibility of avoiding blasphemy. If everything comes from God, evil comes from God — whether the perfect evil of the Devil, the imperfect evil of man, or the impersonal evil of ordinary suffering and death — and the description or denunciation of evil always verges on blasphemy. Moreover the Jewish Bible includes plenty of practical blasphemies — the Fall, when God punished man whom he had created for disobeying an absurd command; the Flood, when God destroyed almost all the living things which he had created because he turned against them; the Exodus, when God persecuted the Egyptians and ordered the Israelites to persecute the Canaanites; the terrible order to kill all Midianite males and married females and to take the rest as slaves (*Numbers* xxxi); the terrible order to kill all the Amalekites, with the punishment of Saul for sparing their king (1 *Samuel* xv); and so on.

From time to time the Jewish Bible itself seems to recognise the blasphemous image of the god it has created, as when God himself is described as saying:

Jehovah, the Lord, a god compassionate and gracious, long-suffering, ever constant and true, maintaining constancy to thousands, forgiving iniquity, rebellion and sin, and not sweeping the guilty clean away — but one who punishes sons and grandsons to the third and fourth generation for the iniquity of their fathers (*Exodus* xxxiv).

Yet somehow the crazy contradictions are accepted and absorbed into a coherent national faith which has survived for three thousand years. Even so, there remain passages in the Bible which are so extreme as to go beyond the bounds of sanity. In the psychopathic ravings of some prophets, God is described as threatening to rub shit on the faces of irreligious priests (*Malachi* ii) and as ordering a prophet to bake bread with human shit (*Ezekiel* iv) — though the latter is allowed on protest to use cowshit instead (if he had been a Hindu, the process would presumably have been reversed).

The book of *Ezekiel* contains perhaps the most amazing passages, in which Israel and Judah are described as whores fornicating with Egypt, Assyria and Babylonia (*Ezekiel* xxiii), or Jerusalem is described as an abandoned girl married by God but fornicating with others (*Ezekiel* xvi). It is God himself who speaks in these passages, and he describes his own sexual participation in first-person narrative in such detail that it is easy to understand why the unexpurgated Bible has been feared by ecclesiastical authorities; it would indeed be hard for an anti-biblical writer to match the blasphemous obscenity of the biblical writers at these points. (This used to be a strong point in Freethought propaganda, and the *Bible Handbook* of G. W. Foote and W. P. Ball, which is still in print more than a century after it was first published in 1888, includes with relish sections not only on 'Bible Atrocities' but on 'Bible Immoralities, Indecencies, and Obscenities'.)

There is also the puzzle of the *Song of Songs*, which seems obviously to be an erotic drama or series of poems but which was seriously attributed to King Solomon and somehow included in the canon of the Bible. The Jewish rabbis solved the puzzle by suggesting the allegorical interpretation of the book as a metaphorical expression of the love of God for Israel, a parable which is at the same time poetically beautiful and sexually explicit. (Consider *Song* v, 4, where the literal translation is: 'My beloved put in his hand by the hole and my bowels moved within me.')

Christian scholars followed this tradition, with the substitution
of Jesus for God and of the Church for Israel. Thus the Vulgate
translation of the Bible into Latin adds a preface to this book: 'This
song is all mystical, very full of the incomprehensible love of Christ
towards his bride, and of the bride towards the bridegroom Christ.'
The Authorised Version of the Bible in English adds headnotes
giving the same message in detail. Thus Chapter v is glossed as
follows: 'Christ awaketh the Church with his calling. The Church,
having a taste of Christ's love, is sick of love. A description of
Christ by his graces.' All this seems very simplistic now, and
modern biblical critics generally agree that the book consists of
erotic verse which may have been connected with fertility rites
but which has no other religious connotation. Yet its presence in
the Bible sanctioned the use of sexual imagery in Judaeo-Christian
religious writing, and its influence may be traced in mystical
literature hundreds or even thousands of years later.

★   ★   ★

One obvious escape-route from the blasphemous implications of
monotheism is polytheism or animism — the theory that there are
many different gods or spirits, who may be either good or bad or
both good and bad, and who share among them the responsibility
for the nice and nasty things in the universe. Obvious examples
are the primitive superstitions which are almost universal in
human society, or the so-called 'pagan' religions of ancient Greece
and Rome and of the Celtic, Germanic and Slav peoples before
Christianity, or the overlapping sets of religion which prevailed
in the Middle East before Judaeo-Christian-Islamic monotheism
or which still prevail in India as Hinduism. This kind of system
enables believers to solve the problem of accounting for the evil
of the world by attributing it to various supernatural forces or
superhuman beings without committing blasphemy against any
which might be particularly moral or sensitive.

Another escape-route from monotheism is dualism (or ditheism)
— the theory that the universe is governed by opposite and almost
equal but quite separate powers of good and evil. The best-known
example is the ancient Persian religion attributed to the sixth-
century figure of Zoroaster, who taught that the world is
dominated by the twin principles of light (or good) and darkness
(or evil). In the earliest Zoroastrian Avestas (scriptures) these are
called Spenta Mainyu (holy spirit) and Angra Mainyu (enemy
spirit), and they were later personified as rival deities, Ahura
Mazda and Ahriman.

This Zoroastrianism or Mazdaism was the established faith of the Persian and Parthian Empires in the Middle East for a thousand years, and it is tempting to trace its influence in the Shi'a form of Islam which later prevailed (and still prevails) in Iran. It seems to have influenced the ancient Jewish religion — hence the increasingly powerful figure of Satan as depicted in successive parts of the Bible — and it is still preserved in a modified form by the Parsis of India.

A revised version of Zoroastrianism was established by the Persian Mani, who was tortured to death in the third century AD, and Manichean dualism had a widespread and long-lasting influence on Christianity. The similar tradition of Gnosticism in the Roman Empire held that the material world was the creation of an evil force, the Demiurge, and that the spiritual world was the sphere of the good force, the Supreme Being, man being a mixture of the two. History, in all these systems, is the record of the cosmic struggle between good and evil, with man in the middle, the final outcome being a triumph of the former over the latter.

Within Judaism the dualist tendency influenced the mysticism of Philo, which was fertile ground for the rise of Christianity, and later influenced the mystical tradition of the Kabbalah. Within Christianity it led to such extreme doctrines as that the God of the Old Testament was the Demiurge and the Redeemer of the New Testament an emanation of the Supreme Being (the basis of the Marcionite sect), or that the material world was utterly evil (the basis of the later Bogomile and Cathar sects). Much later it also influenced Calvinism and Jansenism and the various forms of Evangelical Christianity, with their shared preoccupation with the power of evil in this world.

All these dualistic and other unorthodox tendencies, however, have been at the mercy of the greatest persecuting religion in the world, orthodox Christianity.

★   ★   ★

The revised form of Judaism known as Christianity was established by followers of Jesus in the first century AD. If Jewish history as recorded in the Jewish Bible (the Old Testament) is largely an account of repeated struggles with various kinds of blasphemy by the Jews themselves, the Christian religion as recorded in the Christian additions to the Bible (the New Testament) is even more involved with blasphemy, since it takes its origin from the trial and punishment of Jesus for that very offence (though he is reported to have suffered a Roman rather than a Jewish form of execution). It is a curious fact that two of the most significant figures in our civilisation — Socrates and Jesus — were put to death for blasphemy.

Christianity is indeed both obsessed and permeated with blasphemy. The central events of the Gospels (the Nativity and Crucifixion) and the central doctrines of Christianity (the Incarnation and the Atonement) are profoundly blasphemous both to the Judaism which came before and to the Islam which came after it, because of the repeated confusion of divine and human nature, and the figure of Christ has an ambiguous place as the source of scandal and the symbol of sanctity. (Similar figures subsequently appeared in the Muslim world — al Hallaj, the Sufi mystic who was executed in the tenth century for identifying himself with God, and Sabbatai Tsevi, the Jewish mystic who was forced to become a Muslim under pain of death in the seventeenth century after claiming to be the Messiah.)

In Christianity the theoretical impossibility of avoiding blasphemy is even more acute than in Judaism, since Jesus is meant to have come to destroy evil and save mankind, yet there is no evidence for such an improvement in the world during the subsequent two thousand years and no prospect of a Second Coming to finish the job. And in the Christian New Testament there are plenty more practical blasphemies to add to those of the Old Testament — above all, the new doctrine of damnation, by which those who are not saved for eternal bliss in Heaven are condemned to eternal torment in Hell. Jesus is reported as saying in one Gospel: 'He that believeth not shall be damned' (*Mark* xvi, 16); and in another that mankind will be divided into two, the sheep and the goats, and the latter will 'go from my sight to the eternal fire that is ready for the Devil and his angels' (*Matthew* xxv, 41). Later Christians attempted to soften this harsh eschatology with the doctrine that such punishment would last not for ever but only for a few thousand years, depending on the sins to be expiated. But while this idea of Purgatory may moderate the fear of Hell in theory, it is little consolation in practice.

Apart from the difficulties created by these frightful ideas, there are in the New Testament, as in the Old, passages which must have embarrassed generations of devout Christians for their sexual language. Religious infidelity is again described as fornication and whoredom, and religious fidelity is decribed as marriage and true love. In the Gospels Jesus calls himself the bridegroom of his followers, and some of his later followers developed this theme explicitly and occasionally explosively. The Church has been called the Bride as well as the Body of Christ; nuns are said to enter a 'Spiritual Marriage' with Christ; and in the emotional period of the Reformation and Counter-Reformation there were many mystics, both Catholic and Protestant, who took this kind of language to remarkable lengths.

In Catholic Spain, Teresa of Avila in prose and John of the Cross in poetry described the relationship of the mystic with God as if they were sexual lovers, and the ecstasy of the mystic's union with God as if it were a sexual orgasm. (Teresa added a Freudian element with her vision of an angel with a fiery dart repeatedly piercing her heart at the moment of climax — as shown to great effect in Giovanni Bernini's sculpture.) In Lutheran Germany, Jakob Boehme similarly decribed how he was 'embraced with divine love as a bridegroom embraces his bride'.

This extravagant language entered English literature with the 'Anglo-Catholic' metaphysical poets of the seventeenth century, such as Richard Crashaw and Thomas Traherne, and the great John Donne. Donne's later religious poems contained passages which echo his earlier erotic poems in more than literary technique. His sonnet about the Church, 'Show me, dear Christ, thy spouse', ends as follows:

> Betray, kind Husband, thy spouse to our sights,
> And let mine amorous soul court thy mild dove,
> Who is most true and pleasing to thee then
> When she's embraced and open to most men.

And his sonnet to God, 'Batter my heart, three-personed God', ends as follows:

> Yet dearly I love you and would be loved fain,
> But am betrothed unto your enemy;
> Divorce me, untie, or break that knot again,
> Take me to you, imprison me, for I
> Except you enthral me never shall be free,
> Nor ever chaste except you ravish me.

Such verbal imagery was not seen to be blasphemous, but similar visual imagery was a different matter. Michelangelo's use of openly sexual material in religious art was found excessive, and in a famous — or infamous — episode the more explicit details of the magnificent Sistine frescoes which he painted for one Pope were painted over after his death on the orders of another.

Christian use of such imagery has actually been very restrained in comparison with the high level of eroticism reached by Tantric writers and artists in Hinduism and Buddhism and by Sufi writers in Islam, for whom the idiom of the *Song of Songs* would seem a normal element of religion rather than an abnormal embarrassment (though Jewish and Muslim art was more severely restricted by the ban on any representation of living beings).

The use of sexual imagery has generally been thought blasphemous only when it has been clearly used to attack religion. A good example from British usage is Thomas Potter's *Essay on Woman*, a pornographic parody of Alexander Pope's *Essay on Man* (1733) which was printed in 1763 by the radical politician John Wilkes. Pope had written:

> O blindness to the future! kindly given,
> That each may fill the circle marked by heaven;
> Who sees with equal eye, as God of all,
> A hero perish, or a sparrow fall,
> Atoms or systems into ruin hurled,
> And now a bubble burst, and now a world.
> Hope humbly, then, with trembling pinions soar;
> Wait the great teacher Death, and God adore!
> What future bliss, he gives thee not to know,
> But gives that hope to be thy blessing now.

This was parodied as follows:

> O blindness to the future! kindly given
> That each may enjoy what fucks are marked by Heaven:
> Who sees with equal eye, as God of all,
> The man just mounting, and the virgin's fall;
> Prick, cunt and ballocks in convulsions hurled,
> And now a hymen burst, and now a world.
> Hope humbly, then, clean girls, nor vainly soar;
> But fuck the cunt at hand, and God adore.
> What future fucks, he gives thee not to know,
> But gives that cunt to be thy blessing now.

No wonder this poem was one of the items in the Government's action against Wilkes, involving his outlawry in 1763 and his fine and imprisonment in 1768. But this case brings us to the English law of blasphemy, which must be discussed in the light of the Christian persecution of heresy.

3 Heresy & Persecution

The first Christians didn't expect the world to last long enough to give time for new laws, so the New Testament contains no clear rules about how religious offences were to be treated. Jesus was actually recorded in the Synoptic Gospels as saying that all blasphemy should be forgiven — except that obscurely described as being 'against the Holy Spirit'. The only relevant guidance was given by Paul: 'A man that is an heretic, after the first and second admonition reject' (*Titus* iii, 10); but while the expulsion of dissenters from a small community is one thing, their excommunication from a national Church is quite another, especially when it is reinforced by social ostracism and State punishment. Later apologists for persecution also relied on the parable text, 'Compel them to come in' (*Luke* xiv, 23). The result was one of the darkest chapters in human history.

Christianity began as a blasphemy against Judaism, and the first Christian martyr, Stephen, was punished under the Jewish law. Christianity then became a blasphemy against the pagan religion of the Roman Empire, and later Christian martyrs were punished under the similar Roman laws. For more than two centuries Christians were cruelly persecuted — even under the most enlightened Emperors, such as Marcus Aurelius — and they therefore advocated freedom of religion; at the same time they quarrelled bitterly among themselves about the details of their own religion, and anathematised rival doctrines as damnable heresies.

When the Roman Empire finally became Christian, under Constantine in the early fourth century, the usual pattern prevailed. Not only were non-Christians cruelly persecuted in their turn, but Christians began to persecute each other as well; indeed, said the historian Edward Gibbon, they 'inflicted far greater severities on each other than they had experienced from the zeal of infidels'. Heresy (from the Greek *hairesis*, choosing an opinion, then a false opinion), which meant holding views about Christianity which were different from those of the established authorities, became a more serious offence than paganism, which meant following the old polytheistic or mystery religions. In this context blasphemy was generally seen as a minor

aspect of the major challenge of heresy or unbelief, involving
offensive language as well as dangerous ideas.

One of the first events in the Christian Empire was the bitter
dispute between Arians and Athanasians over the nature of Jesus,
which led to their mutual and sometimes fatal persecution as
heretics throughout the fourth century; and as the various
Churches strengthened their position in the State they suppressed
all rival doctrines, whether Christian or non-Christian. The first
official laws against both paganism and heresy appeared in 380
in the code of Theodosius (the Emperor who had the great library
of Alexandria destroyed), and the first official executions of
heretics were recorded in 385. They were followed by literally
millions of other victims, and during its long reign as an established
faith Christianity claimed more violent deaths than any other
religion; indeed no system of any kind has equalled the terrible
record of persecution inflicted on infidels, pagans, heretics,
witches, and Jews through inquisitions and crusades, through
propaganda, harassment, imprisonment, torture, and death by the
Christians over a millennium and a half.

The persecution of heretics was supported by almost all
medieval Christian thinkers, including the greatest — from
Augustine of Hippo in the fifth century to Thomas Aquinas in the
thirteenth century — and most of them (though not Augustine)
agreed that the punishment should be death. The theoretical
justification was that obstinate heresy was a form of blasphemy;
the practical reason was that Christian authorities were terrified
and infuriated by any kind of disagreement about religion. At all
events, there was a general equation of and overlap between
heresy and blasphemy. Blasphemy was specifically made a capital
offence in the Eastern Empire by the code of Justinian in the sixth
century and in the Western Empire under Charlemagne in the
early ninth century, and for a thousand years it was normally
punished in every Christian state by death. This harsh treatment
didn't apply to clerical blasphemy (private jokes between insiders)
or to popular blasphemy (acceptable humour in miracle and
mystery plays or in profane festivals). It applied mainly to extreme
criticisms of or comments on orthodox beliefs which were
considered insulting to God and dangerous to the stability of both
Church and State.

★   ★   ★

The attitude of Judaism to blasphemy may have remained
unchanged in theory, but in practice Jews had virtually no political

power anywhere for nearly two thousand years, so the only punishment left was expulsion from the community — as happened to many dissenting or freethinking Jews in many places (such as the philosopher Baruch Spinoza in Amsterdam in 1656).

The attitude of Islam, which was founded by Muhammad in the seventh century as a monotheistic reform movement among pagan Arabs under the influence of the Judaeo-Christian religion, was rather different in theory but not so very different in practice from that of Christianity. The *Koran*, which Muhammad claimed was revealed to him by the Archangel Gabriel from a record in Heaven of the word of Allah, is as full of commands as the books attributed to Moses in the Jewish Bible, but there is no law in it against heresy or blasphemy. The faithful are frequently ordered to have nothing to do with infidels and apostates, who will be punished by Allah in Hell, and no secular penalty is mentioned. Yet Islam came into being through the persecution of other religions, and Muslim law soon filled the gap with punishments for religious as for other offences. Islam also split very soon into rival sects — especially the Sunni and the Shi'a — and Muslims followed the pattern of persecuting each other as well as outsiders.

Islam thus became a great proselytising and persecuting religion, like Christianity, though it never managed to match the record of its rival, and for more than a thousand years all Muslim states normally punished apostasy, heresy and blasphemy with death (for men — women were imprisoned). Indeed some have continued to do so — as may be seen from the treatment in Iran of the Babis and then the Baha'is, who seceded from Islam in the mid-nineteenth century and have been ferociously persecuted ever since, or in Pakistan of the Ahmadis, who have suffered a similar fate since the late nineteenth century.

Here it is necessary to consider another form of blasphemy. What is generally thought of as an attack of some kind committed by a powerless individual or minority against a powerful establishment may also appear as an attack of a quite different kind committed by a powerful establishment against a powerless individual or minority.

Thus the Jews, who allowed no criticism of their god, included in their Scriptures violent attacks on their neighbours' gods. The Christians, who were originally called atheists because they rejected the pagan deities of the established religion in the Roman

Empire, later took their revenge when theirs became the
established religion, and they began attacking the old deities in
turn. Thus the most important thinker in the early Christian
Empire, Augustine, filled much of his most important book,
Concerning the City of God Against the Pagans, with repetitive
and abusive attacks on the Greco-Roman gods and goddesses; they
were treated not as false deities but as real demons, and were
described in the most unpleasant terms at a time when they were
still worshipped by many if not most of the population of the
Empire. This kind of blasphemy reinforced the Christian campaign
against paganism, which was eventually suppressed by force
rather rather than supplanted by faith.

In much the same way Islam, which began with blasphemies
against the Arab deities and treated their worship as blasphemy
against the one true deity, suppressed polytheism just as
Christianity had done, with ridicule as well as repression. In most
Muslim states, so-called idolaters and infidels have been treated
very harshly, while Jews and Christians (and Parsis) have been
treated relatively leniently. Nevertheless, Christianity and Islam
both involve blasphemies against Judaism and also against one
another, and when they became powerful faiths they both used
deliberate blasphemy as a weapon in their battles against Judaism
and each other. Mutual insults punctuated the long rivalry
between the two great political religions all the way from Spain
to India, and while Muslims revered Jesus as a prophet (though
they denied that he either was the son of God or had died on the
Cross), Christians represented Muhammad in highly derogatory
ways.

This was a reaction not just to theological differences but to
political disasters suffered when half of Christendom was
conquered by the Muslims within a century of Muhammad's death
and when the Christians failed to recover the lost territories during
the Crusades a few centuries later — traumatic defeats which
could be explained only by invoking divine or diabolical
intervention, and which gave rise to a tradition of prejudice that
has lasted until today.

For a long time Western Christendom knew little about Islam.
Muhammad was often represented as a Christian heretic or
apostate, sometimes a traitorous saint or bishop, and was later
transformed into a fallen angel or devil or even the Antichrist.
At the same time the Muslims were represented as pagans who
worshipped polytheistic deities. Thus the Old French epic *Song
of Roland*, which was written during the eleventh-century

Crusades but set in ninth-century Spain, says in the first stanza that the Muslim king of Zaragoza doesn't love God but 'serves Mahumet and worships Appolin' (*'Mahumet sert e Appolin recleimet'*). 'Appolin' was a corruption of Allah, confused both with the Greek Apollo and with the Christian Apollyon — the name given to the angel of the 'bottomless pit' (*Revelation* ix) and later to the 'foul fiend' in John Bunyan's *Pilgrim's Progress* (1678). 'Mahumet' was similarly corrupted into a mysterious figure called 'Mahound', who appeared very widely in European literature — including Geoffrey Chaucer's fourteenth-century *Canterbury Tales* and Edmund Spenser's sixteenth-century *Faerie Queene* — as a false god or devil, and took the latter part in miracle plays. An indication of the Christian attitude may be seen in the definitions given by the *Oxford English Dictionary* to *Mahound*: 'The "false prophet" Mohammed'; 'A false god; an idol'; 'A monster; a hideous creature'; 'A name for the devil'. And there are similar definitions for *Maumet*.

A good example of this blasphemous treatment of Muhammad appears in one of the best-known works of Christian literature, Dante's fourteenth-century poem, *The Divine Comedy*. Canto 28 of the *Inferno* describes the Ninth Pit of the Eighth Circle of Hell, in which Dante places the 'sowers of scandal and schism', and where he finds Muhammad. A literal translation of the relevant passage runs as follows:

No cask, by losing board or stave,
  Gapes as much as one whom I saw,
  Ripped from chin down to where one farts:

Between his legs hung his guts,
  The vitals appeared, and the wretched sack
  Which makes shit of what is swallowed.

While I was quite absorbed in seeing him,
  He looked at me, and with his hand opened his breast,
  Saying: 'Now see how I tear myself;

See how Mahomet is mangled ....'

This is a fairly mild specimen of Christian controversial style during the Middle Ages; Muslim language about Christianity was generally far more polite.

More than four centuries later, Voltaire faithfully reproduced the old prejudices in his play *Mahomet* (1742), later called *Fanaticism, or Mahomet the Prophet,* and in the English

translation *Mahomet the Impostor* (1744). This made Muhammad
the villain of a melodramatic tragedy in which he is described as
a false prophet, impostor, rebel, usurper, traitor, tyrant, robber,
monster, madman, savage, assassin — and blasphemer. Elsewhere
Voltaire called him 'Tartuffe in arms' (referring to Molière's play
about a religious hypocrite), though he treated the subject more
seriously in his historical writings. *Mahomet* was successfully
performed in France until the authorities noticed its real meaning
and suppressed it as a 'satire against the Christian religion';
Voltaire retaliated in 1745 by dedicating it to Pope Benedict XIV,
who accepted 'with great pleasure', which neatly routed his
enemies!

In a similar way, whereas Islam was generally as tolerant of Jews
as of Christians, Christendom was frequently very intolerant of
Jews as well as of Muslims. Even when they were allowed rights
of residence, throughout the Middle Ages and afterwards they
were often subjected to humiliating public disputations in which
their religion was insulted and after which they sometimes
suffered worse persecution. This religious anti-Judaism easily
developed into racial anti-semitism, which disfigured Christendom
for more than a thousand years, was adopted by the Inquisition,
continued by the Reformation, and inherited by later political
movements; it was also expressed by many otherwise enlightened
writers (including Voltaire).

But the form of Christian persecution which is more relevant
here is that of Christian heresy — of Christians who dissented from
the form of Christianity which prevailed in their societies.

★   ★   ★

As we have seen, heresy existed within Christianity from the
beginning, and was persecuted as soon as Christians won political
power. In most Christian countries there was at least a theoretical
separation of Church and State — the former deciding what was
heresy, the latter putting the decisions into force — and religious
offences were normally prosecuted in ecclesiastical courts and
then punished by the civil authorities (often following a
hypocritical plea for mercy).

As heresy and blasphemy became an increasingly serious
problem in Western Christendom during the growing reform
movements of the later Middle Ages, the main method of treating
heretics or blasphemers was an investigation involving
interrogation and torture by the Holy Office (the Inquisition,
which was formed by the Papacy in the thirteenth century), a

hearing in an ecclesiastical court followed by conviction and excommunication, and the transfer of the case to the civil authorities for imprisonment or execution — the latter often involving burning. A famous example is the case of Joan of Arc in Rouen in 1431, which is vividly described in Bernard Shaw's play *Saint Joan* (1922). At times, however, the persecution of heretics took the form of total war, as in the so-called Albigensian Crusade against the French Cathars in the thirteenth century, or of mass terror, as in the campaign by the Inquisition against the Spanish Muslims and Jews in the sixteenth and seventeenth centuries.

This frightful method of conducting religious controversy reached a climax during the period of the Reformation and Counter-Reformation, when rival sects engaged in bitter struggles all over Central and Western Europe. The process began in Bohemia during the fifteenth century; the persecuted followers of John Hus, who was burnt as a heretic in 1415, gained political power for a time, split into rival sects which began to persecute each other, and united in persecuting more extreme heretics than themselves (their successors were the Bohemian and Moravian Brethren). This pattern was repeated during the sixteenth century, after Martin Luther and Huldrych Zwingli seceded from the Catholic Church and established Protestantism in Germany and Switzerland in the 1520s, followed by John Calvin in the 1530s; it then spread from country to country. For more than a century Catholics and Protestants killed each other, Protestants killed other Protestants, and both Catholics and Protestants killed more extreme dissenters — such as Anabaptists (who opposed all established denominations and had radical ideas about politics as well as religion) and Unitarians (who denied the divinity of Jesus and stressed the unity of God), some of whom raised the idea of universal toleration. The Protestants, whether they followed Luther or Zwingli or Calvin or anyone else, were just as severe with their opponents as the Catholics; for example, they often banned the Mass as a blasphemy on pain of death. Even the best spirits of the age, such as Erasmus and Thomas More, believed that heretics should be killed. Much of Europe was seized with terror and drenched with blood. Some of the victims were well known — Michael Servetus (burnt in Geneva in 1553), Giordano Bruno (burnt in Rome in 1600), Lucilio Vanini (strangled in Toulouse in 1619). Some were more than just well known — Galileo Galilei, the greatest scientist of the age (imprisoned in 1633 and forced to recant his unorthodox views of the universe), and

Spinoza, the greatest philosopher of the age (not only expelled from his Jewish congregation but condemned by both Catholics and Protestants). But most of the victims were unknown apart from their fates.

In the end the various factions gradually fought one another to a standstill and unwillingly accepted a practical truce. As Gibbon said, 'The nature of the tiger was the same, but he was gradually deprived of his teeth and fangs.' Meanwhile, in the midst of this painful process, the first clear and consistent arguments for universal religious toleration were made during the 1550s and 1560s by the French and Italian humanists Sebastian Castellio and Jacob Acontius (and this was extended to unbelievers by the Dutch humanist Dirck Coornhert in 1590). However, it took a long time for such toleration to become practical and general. Heretics and blasphemers were still being killed in several places well into the eighteenth century. In France, for example, one of the cases which involved Voltaire was the execution of Jean de La Barre for insulting a religious procession in Abbeville in 1766; but religious toleration followed the upheavals of the Revolution. Elsewhere the old tradition lasted longer. In Catholic Spain, at one end of Europe, the Inquisition continued to kill its victims (mainly Protestants and Jews) until the early nineteenth century, and wasn't abolished until 1834; and religious toleration was formally declared only in 1869. In Tsarist Russia, at the other end of Europe, the Old Believers were cruelly treated in the eighteenth century, other dissenting sects were persecuted into the twentieth century, and Leo Tolstoy was excommunicated for his unorthodox religious ideas as late as 1901. This tradition of religious persecution laid the foundations for modern political persecution.

One semantic effect of the Reformation was that Protestants, whom the Catholics repeatedly accused of heresy, came to dislike the term, and preferred to accuse their more extreme opponents of blasphemy. As a result, in Protestant countries the harsh persecution of heresy was largely replaced by the milder persecution of blasphemy, though the content of the objectionable material was much the same. Britain is a good example of this pattern.

4 Heresy in Britain

In Britain heresy and blasphemy didn't become a problem until
the late Middle Ages, and legalistic rather than terroristic methods
prevailed. There were laws against 'heathens' and 'heretics' from
before the Norman Conquest, but very few heretics were recorded
before the fourteenth century. The most important was John
Wyclif, whose opposition to the Roman Catholic Church
anticipated Protestantism. He died in 1384 before he could be
condemned, and the heresy laws were then used against his
followers, the Lollards. The system of dealing with them was
formalised from 1401 by a series of statutes with the general title
De Haeretico Comburendo, under which heretics who were
convicted by the ecclesiastical authorities and remained
unrepentant were burnt to death in public by the civil authorities.
Several hundred people were accused of heresy during the next
century or so, and about fifty were actually burnt. Several of the
cases also included blasphemy.

The Reformation in England was more of a political than a
religious business, but it was accompanied by the same pattern
of persecution as on the Continent. Lollards continued to be
persecuted until the 1530s; then in rapid succession Protestants
and Catholics were persecuted under Henry VIII, Catholics were
persecuted under Edward VI, Protestants were persecuted under
Mary, and Catholics and extreme Protestants were persecuted
under Elizabeth. The reign of terror reached a climax during the
brief Catholic reaction under Mary, when nearly 300 Protestants
were burnt and many more died in prison in four years
(1554-1558). It subsided during the settlement made under
Elizabeth, which attempted to unite all believers in a national
Church. During the next half-century about a dozen Anabaptists
or Unitarians were killed; during the same period nearly 200
Catholics were killed, but mostly for political offences. Two well-
known people got into trouble. The poet and dramatist
Christopher Marlowe was accused of atheism, but he was
murdered in mysterious circumstances in 1593 before being tried;
the writer and adventurer Walter Ralegh was suspected of atheism
at the same time, and this contributed to the unpopularity which
led to his fall from favour under Elizabeth and his trial for treason
and eventual execution under James I in 1618.

Persecution of Anabaptists and Unitarians continued into the seventeenth century, but the death penalty fell into disrepute and disuse. In England religious dissent was increasingly punished only if it had political implications — not so much for words as for deeds, not so much for heresy or blasphemy as for sedition or nonconformity — and cases were increasingly taken over from the ecclesiastical courts by the secular Court of Star Chamber.

Finally, under James I the last heretics were executed in England; in 1612 the authorities burnt two Unitarians, Bartholomew Legate in London and Edward Wightman in Lichfield, amid growing public unease. During the next few years, from 1612 to 1615, the first arguments for religious toleration were published in English (by the Baptist leaders Thomas Helwys, Leonard Busher, and John Murton — the latter even including blasphemers), and the climate of opinion slowly relaxed.

The old tradition lasted a little longer in Scotland, where Catholics and extreme Protestants were persecuted impartially by the rival Episcopalians and Presbyterians. In 1651 Alexander Agnew was hanged in Dumfries for unitarian and even atheist views; in 1681 Francis Borstwick was outlawed but managed to escape arrest; and in 1697 Thomas Aikenhead, a boy of eighteen, was hanged in Edinburgh for deist views — the last known martyr of religious laws in Britain. (The same pattern appeared in the treatment of witches, who were being killed in Scotland for more than half a century after the last executions in England during the 1660s.) The old tradition also lasted longer in New England, especially in Calvinist Massachusetts, where four Quakers were hanged as late as 1661 and the persecution was stopped only by the intervention of the British authorities (and where several dozen alleged witches were executed during the Salem panic of 1691-1692). In 1636 Roger Williams was expelled from Massachusetts for his belief in toleration; he immediately founded Rhode Island, where it was guaranteed, and also wrote one of the most eloquent books on the subject, *The Bloudy Tenent of Persecution for Cause of Conscience* (1644). Toleration also briefly prevailed in Maryland and New York under Catholic rule.

In England the process of toleration was first accelerated, then obstructed, and finally accelerated again during the period of Great Rebellion, Civil War, Commonwealth and Protectorate in the 1640s and 1650s. The collapse of the old regime led to an explosion of religious as well as political dissent; the growth of the new regime first under Parliament and then under the Protectorate led to a new wave of persecution; and the restoration of the old regime led to a brief reaction and in the end to an armistice on almost all matters of religious belief.

The Long Parliament, which destroyed the old regime, abolished the Star Chamber and the ecclesiastical courts in 1641. For the next twenty years the authorities had difficulty in dealing with even the most extreme forms of religious expression, partly because they had failed to put an effective new form of jurisdiction in place of the old one, and partly because there was a genuine and widespread belief in religious liberty which spread to the highest places, including Oliver Cromwell himself. There were difficulties with even the worst heretics and blasphemers, and when Parliament itself considered several major cases — Paul Best (1645-47), John Biddle (1646-52, 1654-55), John Fry (1649-51), William Erbury (1652), and above all James Nayler (1656) — each one raised the problem of what the law was and how it should be enforced, and no satisfactory solution was found.

In 1648 the Presbyterian majority in Parliament passed an Act against 'Blasphemies and Heresies', which punished specific 'blasphemies' (mainly atheist and unitarian doctrines) with death and specific 'heresies' (mainly anti-Calvinist doctrines) with imprisonment; but a few months later the Presbyterians were expelled, and the law was seldom used. In 1650 the purged Parliament passed an Ordinance against 'Atheistical, Blasphemous and Execrable Opinions', which punished various other 'blasphemies' (mainly antinomian doctrines) with imprisonment and banishment. Later in 1650 an Act 'for the Relief of Religious and Peaceable People' guaranteed toleration for all forms of Protestantism not covered by these acts, and in 1653 the Instrument of Government which established Cromwell's Protectorate repeated this guarantee.

The main victims of the penal laws of 1648 and 1650 were various Unitarians, the leading Ranters (Abiezer Coppe and Joseph Salmon), the founders of Muggletonianism (John Reeve and Lodowick Muggleton), and the first Quakers (George Fox and James Nayler). In 1656 Nayler was the central figure in the most notorious religious case of the century. For entering Bristol in blasphemous imitation of Jesus entering Jerusalem, he was brought before the House of Commons and sentenced to be pilloried, whipped, bored through the tongue and branded on the forehead, and then imprisoned; he was lucky to escape with his life — which he did only by a vote of 96 to 82 Members of Parliament — and he died soon afterwards. The most dramatic blasphemers of this period were some of the Ranters, who took their radical interpretations of religion to remarkable lengths. In 1650 William Franklin was arrested for claiming to be Christ, and in 1651 two women were imprisoned for claiming that their sons

were Christ. In 1654 Thomas Tany publicly burnt a Bible in London
and attacked the doors of the House of Commons with a sword
while it discussed Biddle's case; he too was lucky to be only
imprisoned, and also died soon afterwards.

The Restoration of the monarchy in 1660 led to the repeal of
the laws passed during the Interregnum, including those against
heresy and blasphemy and for toleration. The ecclesiastical courts
were revived, though they lost most of their penal powers.
Religious passions later began to subside, and religious persecution
began to decline, though it still continued in extreme cases. In
1663 the libertine dramatist Charles Sedley was prosecuted in the
civil courts for several offences, including blasphemy, following
a drunken display in London. His friend the libertine poet John
Wilmot (Lord Rochester) was well known to be an atheist, but he
never got into trouble for this, and made a famous recantation
before he died in 1680. In 1665 Benjamin Keach was prosecuted
as an Anabaptist, and pilloried, fined and imprisoned. In 1666,
during the moral panic following the Great Fire of London, the
sceptical writer Thomas Hobbes was threatened with prosecution
as a heretic on account of his book *Leviathan,* but he escaped.
There were no further prosecutions, and in 1677 the old law
making heresy a major civil offence was at last repealed in
England and Wales (it lasted in Ireland until 1696). Heresy
remained as a minor ecclesiastical offence — along with
blasphemy, atheism and schism — but in practice it could be used
only against clergymen, and the only punishments were
excommunication and deprivation or suspension from their
livings. Yet prejudice continued. Dissenters might not lose their
lives, but they could still lose their liberty or livelihood. Such great
thinkers as John Milton and John Locke had to conceal their
unitarian views, and their respective books on toleration —
Areopagitica (1644) and the *Letters on Toleration* (1689-1692) —
excluded Catholics and atheists.

During the 1660s and 1670s Muggleton had been prosecuted
several more times, and William Penn had been imprisoned several
times without trial; but the Muggletonians and Quakers both
survived as viable sects. The law was clearly ineffective against
organised dissent, and it was retained only as a way of attempting
to persecute the most offensive forms of propaganda against the
established religion of the country — especially the writings of
the Deists (who denied providence and revelation and believed
in natural or rational religion). The concept and law of heresy and
were replaced by the concept and law of blasphemy.

5 Blasphemy in Britain

When heresy gradually declined and virtually disappeared in Britain, a need was still felt for some legal regulation of religious expression, ostensibly to protect the State as much as the Church, actually to punish whoever could still be punished for religious dissent. The one religious crime which was taken over and kept alive by the civil courts was that of blasphemy. There were similar developments in the areas of sedition on one side and of indecency and obscenity on the other, blasphemy often overlapping with one or the other. All these areas had previously been regulated either by the ecclesiastical courts or by the arbitrary Court of Star Chamber, and as such unpopular forms of jurisdiction declined the sorts of offences they had covered were taken over by the ordinary courts in untidy and unsatisfactory ways, following the traditional English methods of improvisation and confusion.

This was certainly true of blasphemy. The law which emerged was (and still is) complex and obscure. There were statutes covering specific blasphemies (insults to the Sacrament from 1547 and to the Prayer Book from 1548) and there was the so-called Blasphemy Act of 1698 (though this really covered specific heretical opinions — denial of the truth of Christianity, the doctrine of the Trinity and the divine inspiration of Scripture); but they were seldom if ever used, and had all become obsolete long before they were finally repealed during the legal reforms of the 1960s. There was also the lesser offence of profanity, which is to blasphemy rather as indecency is to obscenity, and which was eventually incorporated into such statutes as the City of London Police Act, the Metropolitan Police Acts and the Town Police Clauses Acts, which cover profane speech or publication in public places; but this has seldom been used either.

The crime of blasphemy and blasphemous libel (for written material), as it has actually existed in England and Wales for three centuries, has always been a common law offence — that is, a crime which is not defined in an Act of Parliament and does not appear on the Statute Book, but which was invented and has then been developed by judges in a series of cases reported in official records. The judges usually followed the precedents of previous cases, but they occasionally introduced new interpretations, and the law has gradually changed during its long life. Blasphemy is one of the few offences which have remained almost entirely judge-made laws, and this accounts for most of the difficulties surrounding it. It has been the normal criminal charge first against latter-day Christian heretics, then against non-Christian heretics, and later against the non-religious infidels, secularists and atheists, who came forward in succession from the seventeenth to the twentieth century. It has often been said to punish the manner rather than the matter of the material in question, but this test has been applied only to unorthodox religious or anti-religious propaganda and never to orthodox religious propaganda, so in practice blasphemy has meant particularly offensive heresy. The way this law has survived and operated is one of the most obscure and objectionable aspects of our history during this period.

There have been several hundred blasphemy prosecutions in the civil courts. Such cases have normally been brought by indictment, and since 1842 can only be heard in a higher court. Many of them have been begun not by the authorities but by the various vigilantist groups which emerged at the end of the seventeenth century — the Society for the Reformation of Manners appeared in 1690 — and which have continued until the present day. Almost all of them were successful and led to conviction. Most of the victims were sentenced to short terms of imprisonment, some also to large fines, and a few early victims to the pillory.

In theory the law has been justified by various arguments — that it defends divine honour or deflects divine anger, protects the Church or the State, maintains the fabric of society or the consensus of the community, keeps the peace or prevents disorder, preserves public decency or good taste, protects sensitive feelings or a sense of the sacred. In practice, however, it has been used to maintain orthodoxy — to suppress any material concerning religion which the authorities or vigilantists wish to condemn and which courts and juries will convict — and the real motive is the fear expressed by Francis Bacon, that the 'custom of profane scoffing in holy matters' is a cause of atheism (*Essays*, 1612). There is no reason to believe that any of the material in question represented any tangible threat to anyone or anything, whereas the various prosecutions represented physical and financial persecution of a very unpleasant if very ineffective kind. The permanent existence and occasional employment of the law acted as a long-term deterrent to extreme dissent against the established religion of the country, but the main short-term effect of every single case was not to suppress but to increase the circulation of the offending material. In the end, indeed, the law may have had a justification, for the unorthodox views which it has persecuted

have eventually proved to be so powerful that they are now held
more widely than the orthodox views which it has tried to protect.

A full account of the cases would tell much of the history of
militant Dissent and Freethought in this country, but there is space
to mention only a few of them.

★   ★   ★

The first recorded civil prosecution for blasphemy is that of
Nicholas Atwood as early as 1617, though this case is not entirely
clear. When he made trivial but offensive attacks on the
established religion in Bedfordshire, it was decided that he could
be tried by a civil rather than an ecclesiastical court, on the ground
not so much that what he said was blasphemous as that 'the words
are seditious words against the State of our Church and against
the peace of the Realm'. A more serious case was that of John
Traske, a Puritan clergyman who was so fundamentalist that he
returned to the Judaism of the Old Testament. He frequently got
into trouble with the Church authorities because of his
unorthodoxy, and in 1618 he was tried by the Star Chamber not
so much for heresy or blasphemy as for the seditious tendencies
of his propaganda. He was sentenced to be whipped and pilloried,
bored in the ear and branded on the forehead, fined and
imprisoned. (He later moved on to other heresies, but his
followers, the Traskites, became one of the judaising sects whose
modern successors are the Seventh Day Baptists and Seventh Day
Adventists.) There were a few similar cases during the next half-
century, and their line of argument was made formal and
permanent by the otherwise relatively insignificant case of John
Taylor in 1676. Taylor, who seems to have been mentally
unbalanced, was prosecuted for making such remarks in Guildford
as 'Religion is a cheat and profession is a cloak', 'I fear neither
God, Devil nor man', 'I am a younger brother to Christ, and angel
of God', 'Christ is a bastard', 'Christ is a whoremaster', 'God damn
and confound all gods', and so on. He was fined, imprisoned and
pilloried, after claiming in vain that he hadn't meant his words
literally, and disappeared from history.

His case became significant because during it the Lord Chief
Justice, Matthew Hale (who also confirmed the laws against
witchcraft), was reported to have justified the jurisdiction of the
civil courts over blasphemy by declaring that 'such kind of wicked
blasphemous words were not only an offence to God and religion,
but a crime against the Laws, State and Government', that
'Christianity is a parcel of the laws of England', and that

'therefore to reproach the Christian religion is to speak in subversion of the law'. All the blasphemy cases during the following three centuries derived from this judgement; and for two centuries Hale's oppressive and even absurd dictum that Christianity is the law of the land (which derived from the principle established in the fifteenth century that the English common law was based on Scripture, which had been emphasised in several treason trials during the seventeenth century), and that any attack on Christianity is therefore an attack on the State, was used as the basis for such prosecutions.

Meanwhile the Toleration Act of 1689, one of the measures establishing the Whig settlement after the 'Glorious Revolution' which replaced the Catholic James II by the Protestant William and Mary, legalised Protestant Nonconformity and superseded the laws against most unorthodox forms of religious belief and behaviour. This measure at last recognised religious pluralism (just as the contemporary rise of the party system at last recognised political pluralism), but it didn't cover all forms of religion — its protection was later extended to Unitarians in 1813, to Roman Catholics in 1829-1832, and to Jews in 1846 — and the blasphemy law was soon used against some of the more extreme ones. Another significant development was the ending of the Licensing Acts in 1695, which abolished the prior censorship of books, so that they could only be prosecuted after publication rather than suppressed beforehand. (The prior censorship of stage plays was confirmed in 1737 and lasted until 1968; the prior censorship of cinema films was established in 1912 and still exists, being extended to video films in 1984.)

English law applied to British colonies, and most of the countries which are or have been part of the British Empire still have blasphemy laws based on English common law and practice. Thus similar laws were made in most of the American colonies, though some were more severe (as in Massachusetts) and some were more lenient (as in Rhode Island). After Independence, despite the constitutional guarantee of freedom of expression and ban on any establishment of religion, further laws were passed in various parts of the United States, and later there were several blasphemy cases resembling those in the home country.

Scottish law is similar to but separate from English law. Blasphemy was a common law offence in Scotland, as in England, but a more serious one. Acts of 1661 and 1695 specified capital punishment for it, and although this was never imposed after

Aikenhead's case in 1697 they remained in force for more than a century.

These various blasphemy laws were used in the English-speaking world from the late seventeenth century onwards not so much against genuinely offensive material which might cause public disorder as against controversial material which annoyed the authorities and which couldn't be successfully controverted in any other way. When the orthodox couldn't win an argument about religion with words through argument, in fact, they tried to win by force through the law.

In Scotland and America, as we have seen, there were a few cases and even executions before 1700, and there were a few cases afterwards. In Scotland William Dudgeon and Francis Hutcheson were prosecuted for deist views in ecclesiastical courts during the 1730s, and several other people (including Adam Smith and David Hume) suffered discrimination but not prosecution for their known scepticism. In America prosecutions were generally avoided by the simple method of moving to another place.

Back in England there were no executions but there were many more cases. Unorthodox books were often condemned by the English, Scottish or Irish Parliaments. In 1683 Charles Blount's deist writings were condemned, and he escaped prosecution only through the influence of his family and then his death. In 1695 John Locke's unitarian book The *Reasonableness of Christianity* was widely condemned and was lucky to escape prosecution. In 1696 John Toland's deist book *Christianity Not Mysterious* had a narrower escape; it was condemned in both England and Ireland, and he avoided prosecution only by going into hiding and then exile. In 1698 the Blasphemy Act was passed against various specific doctrines, and although it doesn't seem to have been used, as we have seen, it was useful in deterring extreme dissent. It specifically protected the Trinity, but it was amended on its way through Parliament to refer only to people who had once been Christians, in order to save Jews (who were then becoming important in the community); in 1813 it was further amended to remove the reference to the Trinity, in order to save Unitarians (who were then becoming important in the community).

Prosecutions continued sporadically during the eighteenth century. In 1703 Thomas Emlyn, the first Unitarian minister in Britain, was prosecuted in Ireland for his *Humble Inquiry into the Scripture Account of Jesus Christ* and was fined and imprisoned for two years. In 1706 Matthew Tindal's deist book *The Rights of the Christian Church Asserted* was suppressed, but he escaped prosecution. In 1713 Anthony Collins' deist book *A Discourse of Freethinking* was condemned but not prosecuted. In 1721 William Wake, the Archbishop of Canterbury, tried in vain to introduce a stricter Blasphemy Bill into Parliament. In 1726 there was a rare acquittal in the case of Edward Elwall, who was prosecuted in Stafford for his unitarian book *A True Testimony for God and His Sacred Law,* but was freed despite his refusal to withdraw it. In 1728 Thomas Woolston was prosecuted for his deist *Discourses on the Miracles of our Saviour,* in which he denied the literal truth of the miracles of the New Testament, and he was detained until he died in 1733. The judge in his case made the important though ambiguous statement: 'We do not meddle with any differences in opinion; we interpose only when the very root of Christianity itself is struck at.' This was a distinction in theory which made little difference in practice. In 1756 Jacob Ilive was imprisoned for publishing a deist book. In 1758 the Irish bishop Robert Clayton would have been prosecuted for unitarianism if he hadn't died first. In 1763 Peter Annet was prosecuted for his deist magazine *The Free Inquirer,* in which he denied the divine inspiration of the Pentateuch, and was imprisoned and pilloried at the advanced age of seventy. Also in 1763 blasphemy was one of the many counts in the Government's case against John Wilkes.

The application of the law was partly a matter of class. Ordinary clergymen and politicians might suffer, but unorthodox poets like John Dryden or Jonathan Swift, unorthodox aristocrats like Lord Bolingbroke and Lord Shaftesbury, and unorthodox intellectuals like Edward Gibbon and David Hume escaped such treatment for their equally subversive writings. A century later, of course, the views of the Bible for which Woolston and Annet were punished were taken for granted by increasing numbers of intelligent people, including many devout Christians, and were published with impunity.

The law was confirmed by William Blackstone in his authoritative *Commentaries on the Laws of England* (1765-1769). He repeated that 'Christianity is part of the laws of England'; and he defined the offence as 'blasphemy against the Almighty, by denying his being or providence; or by contumelious reproach of our Saviour Christ'; also 'all profane scoffing at the Holy Scripture, or exposing it to contempt or ridicule'.

6 Freethought & Radicalism

Until the end of the eighteenth century, virtually all blasphemy cases involved unorthodox Christianity or other forms of religion such as Unitarianism or Deism. From the beginning of the nineteenth century, however, they began to involve various forms of Freethought, defined as the rejection of all arbitrary authority or assumptions about religion and of supernatural religion itself. Indeed the continued persecution of Deism was one of the causes of the drift towards atheism.

★   ★   ★

A new wave of blasphemy prosecutions began at the time of the French Revolution, when radical discussion in Britain again spread to religious as well as political subjects and when Deism began to give way to atheism. An important change in the general law of libel at this time came with the Libel Act of 1792, which made the jury the sole judge of the facts; but this had little practical effect in cases of blasphemous libel, where juries almost always followed their religious prejudices and the direction of the prosecution and the judge.

The best-known figure in the new wave of cases was Thomas Paine, the leading radical writer on both politics and religion. During the 1790s his book *Rights of Man* (1791-1792) was prosecuted as a seditious libel and his book *The Age of Reason* (1794-1795) was prosecuted as a blasphemous libel. Paine wasn't personally affected, since he never returned to Britain after being outlawed in 1792; the victims were the publishers and booksellers who circulated his masterpieces.

In 1796 a cheap edition of *The Age of Reason* was published by the radical leader Francis Place, together with the bookseller Thomas Williams; it was so successful that Williams then produced a new edition of his own, for which he was prosecuted in 1797 by the Proclamation Society (the first of the vigilantist organisations formed by William Wilberforce) and imprisoned for a year. In 1812 a so-called 'Third Part' of *The Age of Reason* (a collection of Paine's later writings on religion) was produced by the radical publisher Daniel Eaton, for which he was imprisoned for eighteen months and pilloried (when he was applauded rather than assaulted by the public). This case was the occasion of Shelley's magnificent pamphlet, *A Letter to Lord Ellenborough*

(1812), addressed to the trial judge. Shelley himself would certainly have been prosecuted for his pamphlet *The Necessity of Atheism* (1811) if it hadn't been immediately and effectively suppressed as soon as it was published — and he was expelled from Oxford University for first producing and then refusing to repudiate it.

In 1814 Eaton and George Houston were prosecuted for publishing the latter's *Ecce Homo*, an English version of Holbach's *Story of Jesus Christ*; Eaton died, but Houston was fined and imprisoned for two years (he was later active in the American Freethought movement).

In 1817 William Hone was prosecuted for publishing seditious and blasphemous libels — political parodies of Anglican prayers and services. He suffered three trials on three successive days, and in a remarkable exception to the normal rule was found not guilty each time, mainly because his offence was political rather than religious, but partly because his defence amused rather than alienated the juries. Many other people had been imprisoned for repeating his offence, and they all had to be released. One of them was Richard Carlile, who became the bravest protagonist in the struggle for a free press.

Carlile, who set up business as a radical publisher and editor in 1817, deliberately set out to defy and destroy the laws against political and religious dissent. He produced all sorts of subversive material, and in 1818 he republished Paine's writings on religion (*The Age of Reason* with the Third Part and other additions), together with similar writings by other writers (American and French as well as British), and in 1819 he was prosecuted by the Society for the Suppression of Vice (the successor to the Proclamation Society). This was the occasion of Shelley's magnificent letter of protest to the *Examiner* (which was not published until 1880).

When Carlile was tried in October 1819, he read out the whole of *The Age of Reason*, and was therefore able to republish it again in the report of what he called his 'Mock Trials'; he was not allowed to read out passages from the Bible which he said were much more objectionable, so he helpfully listed the relevant references instead. He was also tried for publishing the American Elihu Palmer's deist book *Principles of Nature*. When he lost his appeal in November, he was fined a total of £1,500 and ordered to pay sureties of £1,000 (these huge sums were intended to destroy his business), and was sentenced to three years' imprisonment. He refused to pay anything, and was therefore held in prison for six years. He also refused to let his business be destroyed, although the premises were repeatedly ransacked, and with the help of his family and friends he continued to edit his magazines, republish his books, incite further blasphemies — and incidentally to inspire the first organised Freethought movement in Britain, as local support groups became permanent societies in many parts of England and Scotland.

Carlile was followed into court and prison by his wife Jane and his sister Mary Ann, who both got two years (during which Jane had a child), and then by a long succession of shopmen and shopwomen, who insisted on selling the offending books and papers and some of whom also produced their own *Newgate Monthly Magazine* from prison, and by all sorts of other supporters all over the country. Most of these brave people were unknown (one — who drove all the women from the court by reading out the worst passages from the Bible — was unnamed, being prosecuted and imprisoned as 'a man with name unknown', and only later identified as Humphrey Boyle), but some later became well known — especially James Watson, who was imprisoned for a year in 1823 and later took over Carlile's position and became the leading Freethought publisher of the mid-nineteenth century. (There were also some prosecutions in Scotland, notably of James and Robert Affleck who were imprisoned in 1823.)

★ ★ ★

This was one of the epic battles for freedom of expression, and was seen as such at the time. Susannah Wright, who was prosecuted several times and fined and imprisoned for eighteen months in 1822, said: 'I am bold to tell these persecutors, they never can, they never will, put down these publications .... As the blood of the Christian martyrs became the seed of the Christian Church, so shall our sufferings become the seed of free discussion, and in those very sufferings we will triumph over you.' And she was right. The Freethinkers were few but they were too strong to be silenced. In 1825 the authorities and the vigilantists abandoned the struggle; the prosecutions were stopped and the prisoners were released.

Carlile immediately resumed his activities and reprinted all the offending publications. *The Age of Reason* became the most widely circulated Freethought text in English for more than a century (and it is still in print) — although ironically Carlile and several of his colleagues had moved on from its Deism to atheism during their sufferings. As Carlile himself said, 'Thomas Paine was the

first Englishman that struck an honest and well-aimed blow at
the idolatry of the Christian Church', and the survival of *The Age
of Reason* through thirty years of persecution meant that from the
1820s onwards the crime of blasphemy no longer covered the mere
denial of Christian doctrine but had to contain some element of
genuinely abusive or insulting language. This had already been
accepted by the judges in several of the trials of the Carlile circle,
at least in theory. At Carlile's own trial in 1819, the judge asked:
'Is it a work of candid and impartial inquiry into the truth ... or
is it a work of calumny and scoffing?' And at his sister's trial in
1821, the judge asked: 'Is this a temperate discussion or the writing
of a person who attempts not to argue but to vilify and degrade?'
And the legal authority Thomas Starkie had already stated in his
Treatise of the Law of Slander and Libel (1812) that 'the law visits
not the honest errors, but the malice of mankind'.

The trouble was that the judges of what was honest error and
what was malice were always on one side. Examples of malice
on both sides continued during and after the Carlile cases. Thomas
Davison, who was prosecuted in 1820, was repeatedly fined for
contempt of court as well as imprisoned for blasphemy because
of the way he conducted his case. Robert Wedderburn, an
unorthodox Unitarian preacher (of half-Negro descent), was
imprisoned for two years for a blasphemous sermon in 1820; and
Robert Taylor, an eccentric preacher of an allegorical
interpretation of Christianity (who was Carlile's closest associate
in his later semi-Christian phase), was imprisoned for blasphemous
sermons for a year in 1828 and again for two years in 1831.

A more significant example came with one of the works
republished by Carlile — Shelley's anti-religious poem *Queen Mab*,
which had been privately published in 1813 and promptly
withdrawn. Copies soon found their way into the radical
movement (possibly with Shelley's complicity), and Carlile printed
an extract in his paper the *Republican* in 1820. In 1821 the
bookseller William Clark published a pirated edition and refused
to withdraw it; Shelley publicly protested and tried to get an
injunction to suppress it, but privately approved and tried to get
copies sent to him in Italy. Clark was prosecuted by the Vice
Society, and after Shelley's death in 1822 was imprisoned for four
months. But *Queen Mab* quickly became the most widely
circulated of all freethought poems in English, being as it were
the verse equivalent of *The Age of Reason*. (This was one of several
cases where objectionable works by well-known writers were
pirated by radical publishers — the same fate being suffered by

Southey and Byron — and it was established that there is no copyright in obscene, seditious or blasphemous material.)

Queen Mab had one more strange brush with the law of blasphemy. In 1840 Henry Hetherington, the leading Chartist propagandist and publisher, was prosecuted — among many other things — for publishing Charles Haslam's *Letters to the Clergy of All Denominations*, a rationalist critique of Old Testament morality, and was imprisoned for four months. The judge said that an attack on religion was blasphemous 'if the tone and spirit is that of offence and insult and ridicule'. On the advice of Francis Place, the veteran radical (who had published an edition of *The Age of Reason* more than forty years before), Hetherington retaliated by taking out a private prosecution against Edward Moxon, the publisher of the first full editions of Shelley's poems in 1839. Ironically, Moxon had persuaded Shelley's widow Mary (the author of *Frankenstein*) to omit the most anti-Christian passages from *Queen Mab* in the first 1839 edition, but after protests from Shelley's old friends she had persuaded him to restore them in the second 1839 edition (apart from the inadvertent omission of a single line). Despite a long and eloquent speech by the defence counsel, Thomas Talfourd, Hetherington secured a conviction; but he had aimed to publicise the absurdity of the law of blasphemy, not to punish the publisher of the great blasphemous poem, so he didn't apply for sentence — and in 1847 Moxon included the complete *Queen Mab* in the next edition of Shelley's poems without any further trouble.

This was the last successful prosecution of a serious work of literature for more than a century. Talfourd had mentioned equally blasphemous writings by Shakespeare, Milton, Fielding, Richardson, Gibbon and Byron, and appealed: 'Protect our noble literature from the alternative of being either corrupted or enslaved!' The message does seem to have been received, if not quite understood.

It was always taken for granted that the blasphemy law covered only Christianity and not other religions. Another development at this time was the establishment of the principle that the law covered the doctrines and practices only of the Church of England. In 1838 an Anglican priest called Michael Gathercole was tried at York for attacking the Roman Catholic Church in general and a local Roman Catholic nunnery in particular; he was convicted of defamatory libel for the latter but acquitted of blasphemous libel for the former. The judge stated that the blasphemy law did not protect Judaism or Islam 'or any sect of the Christian religion, save the established religion of the country'; it covered only Christianity 'because Christianity is the established religion of the country', and it covered only the Church of England 'because it is the form established by law'. This principle has often been repeated since then but has never been tested again. The same principle was applied in Ireland at the same time; in 1852 a Catholic friar called John Bridgman was found guilty of anti-Protestant propaganda. (Among the awkward implications arising from the disestablishment of the Anglican Church in Ireland in 1871 and in Wales in 1920 was the question whether they continued to be protected by the blasphemy law; and presumably only the established Presbyterian Church is protected in Scotland.)

★   ★   ★

Paine and Shelley, the two authors of the best-known blasphemies of their period, are well known for their other work, and the writings of both of them are easily available in the late twentieth century; but it is worth quoting the passages which were found particularly objectionable in the early nineteenth century.

Paine was not an atheist, like most of his admirers, but a Deist, and the main argument of *The Age of Reason* is that the evidence for God is in Nature rather than in Scripture, and that the word of God is the Universe rather than the Bible, which is in fact a blasphemy against God:

Whenever we read the obscene stories, the voluptuous debaucheries, the cruel and torturous executions, the unrelenting vindictiveness, with which more than half the Bible is filled, it would be more consistent that we called it the word of a demon than the Word of God. It is a history of wickedness, that has served to corrupt and brutalise mankind; and for my own part, I sincerely detest it, as I detest everything that is cruel....

Did the book, called the Bible, excel in purity of ideas and expression all the books that are now extant in the world, I would not take it for my rule of faith as being the word of God, because the possibility would nevertheless exist of my being imposed upon. But when I see throughout the greatest part of this book scarcely anything but a history of the grossest vices and a collection of the most paltry and contemptible tales, I cannot dishonour my Creator by calling it by his name ....

People in general know not what wickedness there is in this pretended word of God. Brought up in habits of superstition, they take it for granted that the Bible is true, and that it is good; they permit themselves not to doubt it, and they carry the ideas they form of the benevolence of the Almighty to the book which they have been taught to believe was written by his authority. Good heavens! It is quite another thing: it is a book of lies, wickedness and blasphemy — for what can be greater blasphemy than to ascribe the wickedness of man to the orders of the Almighty?...

As to the Christian system of faith, it appears to me as a species of atheism — a sort of religious denial of God. It professes to believe in a man rather than in God. It is as near to atheism as twilight is to darkness. It introduces between man and his Maker an opaque body, which it calls a Redeemer, as the moon introduces her opaque self between the earth and the sun, and it produces by this means a religious or an irreligious eclipse of light. It has put the whole orbit of reason into shade ....

Shelley was a great admirer of Paine, and as we have seen he wrote powerful attacks on the prosecutions of two of his publishers. However, he was not a Deist but an atheist, though of a limited kind — when he incorporated *The Necessity of Atheism* into *Queen Mab* as a note on the line, 'There is no God', he added an introductory warning: 'This negation must be understood solely to affect a creative Deity. The hypothesis of a pervading Spirit co-eternal with the universe remains unshaken.' *Queen Mab* accordingly contains a much more aggressive attack on orthodox religion than anything by Paine.

Where Paine tried to rescue true from false religion, Shelley tried to rescue the world from all religion:

> Now, to the scene I show, in silence turn,
> And read the blood-stained charter of all woe,
> Which nature soon, with re-creating hand,
> Will blot in mercy from the book of earth.
> How bold the flight of passion's wandering wing,
> How swift the step of reason's firmer tread,
> How calm and sweet the victories of life,
> How terrorless the triumph of the grave!
> How powerless were the mightiest monarch's arm,
> Vain his loud threat, and impotent his frown!
> How ludicrous the priest's dogmatic roar!
> The weight of his exterminating curse
> How light! and his affected charity,
> To suit the pressure of the changing times,
> What palpable deceit! — but for thy aid,
> Religion! but for thee, prolific fiend,
> Who peoplest earth with demons, hell with men,
> And heaven with slaves!

And where Paine tried to rescue a good God from Jewish and Christian corruption, Shelley tried to rescue mankind from an evil God:

The self-sufficing, the omnipotent,
The merciful, and the avenging God!
Who, prototype of human misrule, sits
High in heaven's realm, upon a golden throne
Even like an earthly king; and whose dread work,
Hell, gapes for ever for the unhappy slaves
Of fate, whom he created in his sport
To triumph in their torment when they fell!

An atheist is burnt for saying, 'There is no God'; Shelley says:

There is no God!
Nature confirms the faith his death-groan sealed:
Let heaven and earth, let man's revolving race,
His ceaseless generations, tell their tale;
Let every part depending on the chain
That links it to the whole, point to the hand
That grasps its term! Let every seed that falls,
In silent eloquence unfold its store
Of argument: infinity within,
Infinity without, belie creation;
The exterminable spirit it contains
Is nature's only God; but human pride
Is skilful to invent most serious names
To hide its ignorance.
                                        The name of God
Has fenced about all crime with holiness,
Himself the creature of his worshippers,
Whose names and attributes, and passions change,
Seeve, Buddh, Foh, Jehovah, God, or Lord,
Even with the human dupes who build his shrines,
Still serving o'er the war-polluted world
For desolation's watch-word; whether hosts
Stain his death-blushing chariot wheels, as on
Triumphantly they roll, whilst Brahmins raise
A sacred hymn to mingle with the groans;
Or countless partners of his power divide
His tyranny to weakness; or the smoke
Of burning towns, the cries of female helplessness,
Unarmed old age, and youth, and infancy,
Horribly massacred, ascend to heaven
In honour of his name; or, last and worst,
Earth groans beneath religion's iron age,
And priests dare babble of a God of peace,
Even whilst their hands are red with guiltless blood,
Murdering the while, uprooting every germ
Of truth, exterminating, spoiling all,
Making the earth a slaughter-house!

Shelley then asks, 'Is there a God?', and replies:

> Is there a God! — aye, an almighty God,
> And vengeful as almighty!

And he puts into the mouth of God bitter accounts of the basic doctrines of the Judaeo-Christian religion:

> From an eternity of idleness
> I, God, awoke; in seven days' toil made earth
> From nothing; rested, and created man:
> I placed him in a paradise, and there
> Planted the tree of evil, so that he
> Might eat and perish, and my soul procure
> Wherewith to sate its malice, and to turn
> Even like a heartless conqueror of the earth,
> All misery to my fame ....
>   One way remains:
> I will beget a son, and he shall bear
> The sins of all the world; he shall arise
> In an unnoticed corner of the earth,
> And there shall die upon a cross, and purge
> The universal crime; so that the few
> On whom my grace descends, those who are marked
> As vessels to the honour of their God,
> May credit this strange sacrifice, and save
> Their souls alive: millions shall live and die
> Who ne'er shall call upon their Savour's name
> But, unredeemed, go to the gaping grave.
> Thousands shall deem it an old woman's tale,
> Such as the nurses frighten babes withal:
> These in a gulf of anguish and of flame
> Shall curse their reprobation endlessly,
> Yet tenfold pangs shall force them to avow,
> Even on their beds of torment where they howl,
> My honour and the justice of their doom.
> What then avail their virtuous deeds, their thoughts
> Of purity, with radiant genius bright,
> Or lit with human reason's earthly ray?

There is plenty more such stuff — no wonder Hetherington got his verdict against Moxon! But there is plenty of similarly offensive material in Burns or Byron, and there are occasional items in other poets from John Keats — the sonnet 'Written in Disgust of Vulgar Superstition' (1816) — to Arthur Hugh Clough — 'The Latest Decalogue' (1862). But the orthodox always preferred to pursue easier game in the Freethought movement.

7 Early Secularism

The growing religious pressure of the early Victorian age caused many members of the radical movement — the Owenites and Chartists — to react by moderating their irreligion; but the more irreligious radicals reacted to this by increasing their attacks on religion and developing what became the Secularist movement. In the process several of the leaders fell foul of the law. The prosecution of Hetherington himself marked the beginning of a new wave of blasphemy cases in the early 1840s, prompted by the Bishop of Exeter, Henry Phillpotts.

In 1841 the Royal Commissioners on the Criminal Law reported that 'the law distinctly forbids *all* denial of the being and providence of God, or the truth of the Christian religion', but that in practice it was used only in cases of 'insulting or contumacious language'. Such language was soon revived. Also in 1841 Charles Southwell in Bristol began the *Oracle of Reason,* an openly atheist weekly paper, and in 1842 he was prosecuted for several articles in it — especially an attack on the Bible in the fourth issue called 'The Jew Book' (the phraseology was anti-Judaic rather than anti-semitic):

That revoltingly odious Jew production, called BIBLE, has been for ages the idol of all sorts of blockheads, the glory of knaves, and the disgust of wise men. It is a history of lust, sodomies, wholesale slaughtering, and horrible depravity, that the vilest parts of all other histories, collected into one monstrous book, could scarcely parallel! Priests tell us that this concentration of abominations was written by a god; all the world believe priests, or they would rather have thought it the outpourings of some devil.

Southwell was fined £100 and imprisoned for a year. While he was in prison his successor as editor of the *Oracle of Reason,* the young G. J. Holyoake, also got into trouble. In 1842 he gave a lecture in Cheltenham on home colonisation, and in question time he was asked by a clergyman planted in the audience what provision should be made for God in the new colonies. There was some dispute about his exact reply, but his own version is as follows:

As you, sir, have introduced religion into this meeting, which I have carefully avoided in my lecture, I will answer your question frankly

and sincerely.... Home colonisation is an economic scheme, and as we
can ill bear the burden of a God here, he may lie rather heavy on their
hands there. Our national debt and our national taxes hang like millstones
round the neck of the poor man's prosperity, saying nothing of the
enormous gatherings of capitalists in addition to all this; and in the face
of our misery and wants we are charged twenty millions more for the
worship of God.... I appeal to your heads and your pockets if we are
not too poor to have a God. If poor men cost the state so much, they would
be put like officers on half-pay. I think that while our distress lasts it
would be wise to do the same thing with the Deity.

He was said to have made further irreligious remarks which might
have been expected to cause greater offence — 'My creed is to
have no creed'; 'All religion has been driven out of me'; 'Religion
has ever poisoned the fountain springs of morality'; 'I shudder
at the thought of religion, I flee the Bible as a viper, and revolt
at the touch of a Christian, for their tender mercies may next fall
upon my head' — but it was the phase about putting God on half-
pay which brought their tender mercies upon his head and for
which he was prosecuted. Carlile himself came to his support, and
sat with him during his trial; but although — or because — he spoke
in his own defence for more than nine hours, Holyoake was
convicted and sentenced to six months' imprisonment. His
daughter died of hunger while he was in jail, and the experience
scarred his life. He repeated his remarks in Cheltenham after his
release, but was not prosecuted again, and he spent the rest of
his long career trying to make freethought acceptable in polite
society.

One of Holyoake's associates at the *Oracle of Reason,* George
Adams, was imprisoned for a month in 1842; but the paper
continued, and the Freethinkers formed an Anti-Persecution
Union to resist the censorship of their publications. In 1843 a new
editor, Thomas Paterson, was fined and imprisoned for a month
for displaying profane material in London. He and Southwell then
moved to Scotland, where the next phase of persecution had
begun.

In Scotland the Acts making blasphemy a capital offence had
been repealed in 1813, and Acts of 1825 and 1837 limited the
penalties to fine and imprisonment, putting it on the same basis
as in England. Thomas Finlay and his son-in-law Henry Robinson
were arrested for selling blasphemous and obscene literature in
Edinburgh, so Southwell and Paterson provocatively sold their
blasphemous literature there and were soon prosecuted as well.
In 1843 Paterson was found guilty by a majority verdict and

sentenced to fifteen months' imprisonment; then Finlay was sentenced to two months' and Robinson to twelve months' imprisonment. Southwell returned to England, but in Scotland Matilda Roalfe continued the work until she was sentenced to two months' imprisonment in 1844; her place was immediately taken by William Baker 'of the United Order of Blasphemers', and the struggle continued.

Each trial was fully reported and each martyr strongly supported, until the pressure on the authorities became as irresistible as in England twenty years before. Roalfe, like many women before and since, showed just as much determination as her male colleagues; her defence speech was reported as follows:

She did not regret what she had done, nor did she believe that she should; she should have no occasion to do so, and so soon as she was at liberty she should consider it her duty to do the same thing again.... The question was not whether Christianity was true or false, but whether Atheists had an equal right with Christians to publish their opinions. She had only to repeat that it was her intention to pursue the same course again, so soon as she should be at liberty.

And she did. Emma Martin, another leading woman Freethinker, spoke in support of her colleagues in both England and Scotland, but although her meetings were harassed she wasn't prosecuted. The persecution of Freethought publishers and speakers continued but, although they lost every case brought against them, by the mid-1840s they had won the right to publicise their ideas by speaking or writing, and the prosecutions ceased.

These were the last known cases in Scotland. Blasphemy remained a common law offence, but private prosecutions are said to be very improbable in such cases. According to the authoritative textbook, Gerald H. Gordon's *Criminal Law of Scotland* (1967, 1978), 'It is extremely unlikely that any prosecutions will now be brought for blasphemy, and it may be said that blasphemy is no longer a crime.' We shall see.

From the mid-1840s the main effort of the Freethought movement was directed to becoming respectable. In 1846 its best-known leader, G. J. Holyoake, started the *Reasoner*; in 1851 he adopted the word *Secularism* to describe its principles and began forming local Secular Societies, and in 1853 he and his brother Austin Holyoake took over Watson's Freethought publishing business. In 1866 the leader of the militant Secularists, Charles Bradlaugh, formed the first countrywide Freethought organisation, the National Secular Society, but despite his reputation he always expressed himself in very moderate terms. However, the Freethought movement never forgot its roots in the bitter struggle for free speech and the free press, and it was still to suffer further persecution from the blasphemy law.

The harassment of Freethought publishers and speakers ran in parallel across the Atlantic, and the American movement like the British depended on its martyrs of persecution — though in the United States the orthodox tended to use the law of obscenity rather than blasphemy. The leading case was that of an obscure Freethinker called Ruggles, who was prosecuted and fined in New York State in 1810 for a speech in which he said that 'Jesus Christ was a bastard and his mother must be a whore'. When he appealed to the State Supreme Court in 1811 on the ground that there was no law of blasphemy, the Chief Justice, James Kent, stated that the English common law was part of American law and that blasphemous words or actions or writings 'continue, as at common law, to be an offence against the public peace and safety' — a ruling which was generally accepted throughout the United States. The main subsequent case was that of the leading New England Freethinker, Abner Kneeland, a popular speaker who founded the *Boston Investigator* in 1831. He was tried in Massachusetts for several articles no fewer than four times in 1834-1835, and spent two months in prison in 1838. There were several other cases at that time, mainly involving small fines or short sentences, and occasionally ending in acquittals or successful appeals. There were a few later American cases. In 1887 Charles B. Reynolds was found guilty of blasphemy in New Jersey for Freethought lectures, despite a very eloquent defence speech by the leading American Freethinker Robert C. Ingersoll, though he got only a small fine. But in 1894 Charles E. Moore, editor of the *Blue Grass Blade*, was acquitted of blasphemy in Kentucky; from 1916 to 1926 Michael X. Mockus was prosecuted in several states for Freethought lectures but never convicted; and in 1926 Anthony Bimba was acquitted. Most of the very few later prosecutions were of religious controversialists rather than Freethought propagandists.

Back in England there was an isolated case of blasphemy in 1857, when a disturbed man called Thomas Pooley was sentenced to twenty-one months' imprisonment in Cornwall for writing on walls and gates incoherent slogans which included abusive references to Jesus and the Bible. This miscarriage of justice was quickly exposed by Holyoake, and Pooley was released after five months. The case was also publicised by two highly respectable

Freethinkers, J. S. Mill (in his essay *On Liberty* in 1859) and
H. T. Buckle (in his review of it in *Fraser's Magazine* in May 1859),
and it was long remembered.

Buckle angrily described the case in great detail, and he
returned to the subject in a pamphlet *Letter to a Gentleman
Respecting Pooley's Case* (1859). 'Shame! shame on it!' he
exclaimed. 'It is a revival of cruelty; it is a revival of bigotry; it
is a revival of the tastes, habits, and feelings of those days of
darkness which we might have hoped had gone for ever.' Mill
more gently described such cases as 'but rags and remnants of
persecution' — 'not so much an indication of the wish to
persecute, as an example of that very frequent infirmity of English
minds, which makes them take a preposterous pleasure in the
assertion of a bad principle, when they are no longer bad enough
to desire to carry it really into practice'. He didn't know that in
1851 the authorities had actually considered prosecuting him for
his irreligious propaganda, or that such persecution would be
revived again.

There were also a few cases of clerical heresy at that time.
Essays and Reviews (1860) was a collection of unorthodox essays
on Christianity. In 1862 two of the contributors were successfully
prosecuted for heresy in the ecclesiastical Court of Arches, and
suspended from their livings; but in 1864 they successfully
appealed to the Privy Council, which was sarcastically said to have
'dismissed Hell with costs'. Similarly, when John William Colenso
began producing unorthodox books about the Old Testament in
1862 he was deprived of his South African bishopric, but he also
successfully appealed to the Privy Council. However, when
Charles Voysey was deprived of his living in 1869 for preaching
against Biblical inspiration, he lost his appeal to the Privy Council
in 1871 (and spent the next forty years leading his own Theistic
Church). Meanwhile much more subversive attacks on orthodox
religion were made with impunity by such intellectual writers as
Herbert Spencer and T. H. Huxley; but the orthodox didn't dare
to proceed against these people, and later turned again on the
organised Freethought movement instead.

8 The Climax of Secularism

The peak of militant Freethought in the late nineteenth century was marked by several blasphemy cases. Bradlaugh, the main leader of the movement, was never prosecuted for blasphemy on account of anything that he himself said or wrote, but his meetings and his papers were frequently harassed on the ground that he might break the law.

This led to a notable battle for the freedom of the press during the late 1860s, when the authorities gave in to a right-wing campaign against his weekly *National Reformer*, which was as radical in politics as in religion. Under the repressive laws which had been passed at the time of Carlile to harass cheap radical publications, Bradlaugh was asked in May 1868 to provide sureties against the appearance of blasphemous or seditious material in his paper. Even if he had been willing to do so, he would not have been able to raise the large amount of money required, and he preferred to attack the authorities in the courts, meanwhile publishing the *National Reformer* with the front-page slogan, 'Prosecuted by Her Majesty's Government'. He won several minor issues, but had no hope of winning the major one, and he soon became liable for penalties totalling several million pounds, when the Press Acts were suddenly repealed in June 1869 as a direct result of his resistance.

There was then another respite for more than a decade — though one of the reasons for the prosecution of Bradlaugh and Annie Besant for reissuing Charles Knowlton's allegedly obscene birth-control pamphlet *Fruits of Philosophy* in 1877 was that it was published by Freethinkers. In 1878 the growth of the movement was marked by the appearance of two pamphlets — Bradlaugh's *The Laws Relating to Blasphemy and Heresy* and W. A. Hunter's *The Past and Present of the Heresy Laws* — which confidently demanded the abolition of the laws. Instead, however, a new wave of blasphemy cases began. In 1882 a young member of the National Secular Society in Tunbridge Wells called Henry Seymour, annoyed by the way local Christians defaced NSS posters, designed a provocative one mentioning among other Easter attractions 'Hamlet and the Holy Ghost'. He refused to remove the word 'Holy' and was prosecuted, but on Bradlaugh's advice he pleaded guilty and was bound over. (Seymour later became a leading anarchist and campaigner for sexual liberation.)

Seymour's case was part of a major attack on the Secularist movement during the early 1880s. Bradlaugh was in the middle of his struggle to get into the House of Commons, after being elected as a Liberal Member of Parliament for Northampton in 1880; he was prevented from either swearing or affirming before taking his seat, and his right-wing and religious opponents were using every trick to keep him out. One would be to prosecute him for blasphemy, because a conviction would disqualify him from holding public office or from taking legal action against his unscrupulous persecutors. They would have liked to prosecute the *National Reformer*, but it was too moderate, so they decided to strike at him through the *Freethinker*, a much more aggressive new paper produced by some of his Secularist colleagues.

In January 1882 they tried to persuade the Government to take action; but the Liberal Home Secretary, William Harcourt, despite his personal feelings followed expert advice and replied: 'It has been the view for a great many years of all persons responsible in these matters that more harm than advantage is produced to public morals by Government prosecutions of this kind. I believe that they are better left to the reprobation which they will meet in this country from all decent members of society.' They therefore decided to take action themselves; and in July 1882 private prosecutions were started against the editor G. W. Foote, the publisher W. J. Ramsey, and the printers — and also against Bradlaugh, whose Freethought Publishing Company shared the same premises as the *Freethinker* and had published the first issues.

Bradlaugh was able to get a separate trial and to show that he had nothing to do with the offending issues of the *Freethinker*, and he was acquitted. But Foote and Ramsey faced three trials in succession in Spring 1883. At the first one before the Catholic judge Ford North, whose prejudice was obvious throughout, the jury disagreed. At the second one before the same judge the jury convicted, and Foote was sentenced to a year's imprisonment, making the classic remark: 'My Lord, I thank you — the sentence is worthy of your creed.' (Ramsey got nine months, and the printer three.) At the third one, before the Lord Chief Justice, John Coleridge, who had prosecuted Pooley twenty-six years earlier but who presided with notable impartiality, the jury again disagreed, and the case was dropped. When Foote was released he returned to the *Freethinker*, which survives to this day; he later succeeded Bradlaugh as president of the National Secular Society, which also survives to this day.

Two significant points in Foote's case were that, unlike Holyoake and Bradlaugh but like Carlile and Southwell, he invited prosecution by deliberately publishing blasphemous material, and that Coleridge's judgement brought a change to the law of blasphemy. Foote said in the first issue:

> The *Freethinker* is an anti-Christian organ, and is therefore chiefly aggressive. It will wage relentless war against superstition in general, and against the superstition of Christianity in particular. It will do its best in this direction, employing the arms of science, scholarship and philosophy against the Bible; and it will not scruple to use for the same purpose any weapons of ridicule or sarcasm which may be derived from the armoury of common sense. (May 1881)

Perhaps the most objectionable material it published was a series of 'Comic Bible Sketches' taken from French books by 'Léo Taxil' (Gabriel Antoine Jogand-Pagès), which were crudely anti-religious and anti-semitic cartoons of appropriate biblical events — very effective, but also very offensive. While the first prosecution was pending, Foote produced a Christmas Number in December 1882, which he himself boasted was 'full from cover to cover of what the orthodox call blasphemy', and which brought another prosecution in January 1883.

That Christmas number of the *Freethinker* may be taken as what was on the edge of blasphemy a century ago, since it was the subject of the two trials in which one jury disagreed and another convicted. It began with a fairy-tale parody of the myth of the Fall and the Atonement, by Joseph Symes, described as 'the Christian Scheme of Redemption, stripped of its pious trappings, writ as it ought to be writ, and exhibited in its gory features and its diabolic qualities'. It contained a hilarious report by J. M. Wheeler of the trial for blasphemy of Matthew, Mark, Luke and John, who

> being wicked and evil-disposed persons did publish or cause to be published certain blasphemous, impious, scurrilous, libellous and scandalous matters, wickedly and profanely devising to asperse and vilify Almighty God and against his honour and dignity, to the tenor and effect following, to wit, among other matters, that he, Almighty God, did cohabit with or overshadow a certain Jewish virgin named Mary, and hocus her affianced husband Joseph, and that, as a result of such overshadowing an illegitimate son named Jesus was born. Concerning whom the defendants alleged divers monstrous, blasphemous and profane libels — to wit, that he, Jesus, was God himself, that he overturned God's

immutable laws, and alleged that the All-Merciful had prepared eternal
torments for those who would not believe in him, the aforesaid Jesus,
and further that such torments were especially prepared for the great
mass of God's creatures on account of sins committed before they were
born ....

The jury's verdict, after some genuinely scholarly evidence, was
that 'there was nothing to prove that the prisoners wrote the libels
complained of'! There were some rather feeble but quite funny
doggerel poems. There was a strip-cartoon 'New Life of Christ',
showing Jesus being 'worshipped by wise ones' (the animals in
the stable), preaching 'from the Mount' (a pub called the Mount
Inn), riding into Jerusalem (like a circus clown on two donkeys),
being 'run in for blasphemy', and so on. And there was the famous
cartoon of 'Moses Getting a Back View' of God, drawn as a man
with his shirt poking through a hole in his patched trousers
(illustrating *Exodus* xxx, 22-23).

It is difficult to imagine any Freethought paper bothering to
publish such stuff now, but it is easy to imagine any Christian
being offended by it then or now. The surprising thing is that Foote
only just went too far — and that he got away with going too far
again, since he continued the 'Comic Bible Sketches' for several
years after his release and never moderated his attacks on
Christianity, but he was never prosecuted again (though the
Freethinker was threatened as late as 1908).

Apart from this Carlilean determination, the strongest point of
his defence was that he described all the technically blasphemous
material written by respectable figures of his time, including
members of both Houses of Parliament and some of the greatest
names in English literature. And he extracted from Coleridge the
important ruling that 'it is no longer true ... that Christianity is
part of the law of the land', as well as a confirmation that 'the
mere denial of the truth of Christianity is not enough to constitute
the offence of blasphemy' and that 'if the decencies of
controversy are observed, even the fundamentals of religion may
be attacked'. Coleridge ruled instead that 'indecent and offensive
attacks on Christianity or the Scriptures or sacred objects or
persons, calculated to outrage the feelings of the general body
of the community, do constitute the offence of blasphemy', so
that the issue must be the manner of expression rather than the
matter expressed.

★   ★   ★

Foote was the last major victim of the blasphemy law for several
decades (though in 1885 Robert Ferguson was briefly imprisoned

for profanity in Glasgow for selling the *Freethinker*), but of course blasphemy did not cease. Apart from the overtly anti-religious items in the *Freethinker* and other Secularist papers, there were more covert writings like those which had been mentioned by Foote in his trials. He pointed out that what Annet and Woolston had been punished for in the eighteenth century was said with impunity in the nineteenth century by respected writers such as Colenso and Arnold; he quoted a passage from Arnold's *Literature and Dogma* ridiculing the doctrine of the Trinity by applying it to three Lord Shaftesburys. (Arnold removed the passage from the next edition of the work on the ground that it might offend Lord Shaftesbury!) He referred to anti-religious passages in the writings of Leslie Stephen, Charles Darwin, T. H. Huxley, Henry Maudsley, John Stuart Mill, George Grote, Jeremy Bentham, John Morley, Lord Amberley, the Duke of Somerset, George Eliot, and so on.

He quoted Herbert Spencer's contemptuous summary of Christian orthodoxy — 'the dogmas that Father, Son, and Holy Ghost are each of them almighty; and yet there are not three almighties but one almighty; that one of them suffered on the Cross and descended into Hell to pacify another of them; and that whosoever does not believe this without doubt shall perish everlastingly'. He quoted Shelley again. But above all he quoted Swinburne — 'one of our greatest, if not our greatest poet' — who had recently been taken under the protection of Theodore Watts-Dunton to save him from his alcoholism but was still writing and publishing poetry which approached obscenity and blasphemy as near as possible without actually being prosecuted. There was indeed a threat that the first volume of *Poems and Ballads* (1866) should be prosecuted for obscenity, and a couple of blasphemous poems were withdrawn from *Songs Before Sunrise* (1871); but *Poems and Ballads* was simply taken over by another publisher, and the poems omitted from *Songs Before Sunrise* appeared elsewhere a couple of years later.

Foote made great play with Swinburne, and he had a great deal to play with. In *Atalanta in Calydon* (1865) there is the famous Chorus attacking 'the supreme evil, God'; in the 'Hymn to Proserpine' (included in the first *Poems and Ballads*), a powerful attack on the suppression of paganism by Christianity, there is a bitter reference to 'ghastly glories of saints, dead limbs of gibbeted gods'; in 'Hertha' (included in *Songs Before Sunrise*), a paean to the pantheistic earth-goddess, there is the exultant conclusion that the Christian god is dying. Foote read out the similar conclusion to the passionately humanistic 'Hymn of Man' (included in *Songs Before Sunrise*):

Kingdom and will hath he none in him left him, nor warmth in his breath;
Till his corpse be cast out of the sun will ye know not the truth of his
                                                                death?
Surely, ye say, he is strong, though the times be against him and men;
Yet a little, ye say, and how long, till he comes to show judgement again?
Shall God then die as the beasts die? who is it hath broken his rod?
O God, Lord God of thy priests, rise up now and show thyself God.
They cry out, thine elect, thine aspirants to heavenward, whose faith
                                                          is as flame;
O thou the Lord God of thy tyrants, they call thee, their God, by thy name.
By thy name that in hell-fire was written, and burned at the point of thy
                                                                sword.
Thou art smitten, thou God, thou art smitten; thy death is upon thee,
                                                          O Lord.
And the love-song of earth as thou diest resounds through the wind of
                                                          her wings —
Glory to Man in the highest! for Man is the master of things.

Foote also read out the passage from 'Before a Crucifix' (included in *Songs Before Sunrise*) which attacks not just God and religion in general but Jesus and Christianity in particular, and which is as blasphemous as anything published in the *Freethinker*:

> O hidden face of man, whereover
>   The years have woven a viewless veil,
> If thou wast verily man's lover,
>   What did thy love or blood avail?
>   Thy blood the priests make poison of,
>   And in gold shekels coin thy love.
>
> So when our souls look back to thee
>   They sicken, seeing against thy side,
> Too foul to speak of or to see
>   The leprous likeness of a bride,
>   Whose kissing lips through his lips grown
>   Leave their God rotten to the bone.
>
> When we would see thee man, and know
>   What heart thou hadst toward men indeed,
> Lo, thy blood-blackened altars; lo,
>   The lips of priests that pray and feed
>   While their own hell's worm curls and licks
>   The poison of the crucifix.

Thou bad'st let children come to thee;
  What children now but curses come?
What manhood in that God can be
  Who sees their worship, and is dumb?
    No soul that lived, loved, wrought, and died,
    Is this their carrion crucified.

Nay, if their God and thou be one,
  If thou and this thing be the same,
Thou shouldst not look upon the sun;
  The sun looks haggard at thy name.
    Come down, be done with, cease, give o'er,
    Hide thyself, strive not, be no more.

Another form of blasphemy which was for some reason immune from the law was what may be called political blasphemy, practised above all by revolutionary anarchists who were also militant atheists. Thus Michael Bakunin's *God and the State*, which inverted Voltaire's famous remark by saying that 'if God existed he would have to be abolished', and Johann Most's *The God Pestilence*, which was full of aggressive abuse, both escaped prosecution when they were published in English — even though the former was published by Henry Seymour himself in the same year as the *Freethinker* trials, and the latter was written by a German immigrant who had been imprisoned for sedition in 1881 (indeed it has been prosecuted on the Continent as late as the 1970s).

9 Later Secularism

Foote's imprisonment was followed by the formation of a Society for the Suppression of Blasphemous Literature, which threatened to prosecute Swinburne and several other respectable Freethinkers; but this was probably a joke, like the prosecution of Shelley's *Queen Mab* forty years earlier. A more serious development was the formation by a group of Freethinkers and progressive Christians of an Association for the Repeal of the Blasphemy Laws — for which W. A. Hunter wrote another pamphlet, *The Blasphemy Laws: Should They Be Abolished?* (1884) — and a campaign for this object during the General Election of 1885. In 1886 Courtney Kenny, a Liberal Member of Parliament, introduced into the House of Commons a Religious Prosecutions Abolition Bill, which would abolish the blasphemy laws and similar provisions, but would replace them with a new law extending legal protection from intentional insult to all religions. This followed the line taken by Thomas Macaulay in Parliament back in 1833 — that 'it is monstrous to see any judge try a man for blasphemy under the present laws' but that it should be illegal to insult any religion (and he later introduced such a provision into the Indian legal code). However, this compromise pleased neither Christians nor Freethinkers, and was abandoned.

James Fitzjames Stephen, the conservative Freethinker and leading jurist (and brother of Leslie Stephen), disagreed with what he called the 'milder view of the law' of blasphemy expressed by Coleridge's interpretation; he believed that it was as restrictive as ever, and he argued in the *Fortnightly Review* (May 1884) that it was so bad that it should be abolished altogether. He prepared a Bill to Abolish Prosecutions for the Expression of Opinion on Matters of Religion which would get rid of the blasphemy laws and similar provisions without putting anything in their place. Bradlaugh, who finally secured his seat in Parliament in 1886, introduced the Bill into the House of Commons in 1889, but it was refused a Second Reading by a vote of 143 to 48. (He was worn out by his struggles, and died in 1891.)

There was a lively controversy both about what the law was and what should be done about it. Whatever the theoretical merits of the respective arguments, the practical outcome of the recent cases was that blasphemy had indeed become a rather milder law, affecting only seriously offensive material, and that it was seldom used any more. There were no further prosecutions by the Government, following the policy declared by Harcourt, and future cases were brought either by local police proceedings or by private prosecutions.

Anyway, by this time the Freethought movement was becoming increasingly respectable. The National Secular Society moderated its militancy, though there were always some more extreme activists (especially those involved in the British Secularist League in the North). The Holyoakes' publishing business, which had been taken over in 1874 by Charles Watts, was handed over in 1882 to his son Charles A. Watts; the latter formed a series of publishing organisations, culminating in 1899 in the foundation of the Rationalist Press Association, with the aged G. J. Holyoake as its first chairman. All the national Freethought organisations united in opposing the blasphemy law and campaigning against it, but none of them set out to defy it any more, though they still sometimes broke it in their publications, however respectable.

★ ★ ★

There was a lull for a couple of decades, though in 1897 J. M. Browne was convicted of sending blasphemous and obscene material through the post, and in 1903 J. W. Gott, George Weir and Ernest Pack were unsuccessfully prosecuted for an article and cartoon in the Bradford Secularist paper the *Truthseeker* (reprinted from the *Freethinker* of 1888). The next — and last — wave of prosecutions ran from 1908 to 1921, coinciding with the wave of political unrest before, during and after the First World War, and involving a dozen cases resulting in fines or short prison sentences for open-air Secularist speakers in London and the industrial Midlands and North.

In 1908 Harry Boulter was bound over and in 1909 he got a month for speeches at Highbury Corner, London. In 1911 J. A. Jackson was bound over by a British court in Shanghai for producing a Chinese translation from an article about Chinese missionaries in the *RPA Annual*. In 1911 J. W. Gott got four months and T. W. Stewart (who called himself Doctor Nikola, after the hero of Guy Boothby's thriller) got three months for speeches and publications in Leeds. In 1912 Thomas Jackson twice got two weeks for speeches in Leeds, and Frederick Chasty and Douglas Muirhead were fined for speeches in Ilkeston (all three charged with profanity rather than blasphemy). In 1913 Edward Stephens (who called himself S. E. Bullock), got three months for a speech in Rotherham, Arthur Thompson was fined £5 for a speech in Blackburn (including the remark that 'when the Lamb of God descended into Hell, the Devil swore because there was no mint sauce with the roast lamb'), and Stewart got another four months for a speech in Wolverhampton. There were some other cases when prosecutions were dropped, and a few when defendants were acquitted. The persecution aroused much anger, and there were widespread protests and petitions against it.

The Freethought movement was reluctant to support such cases, the national organisations opposing both the matter and the manner of the offending speeches, but in 1912 they again joined progressive Christians in forming a Committee for the Repeal of the Blasphemy Laws, which started a successful public campaign. In 1913 a deputation saw the Liberal Prime Minister, H. H. Asquith, who gave his sympathy. In 1914 the Liberal Attorney General, John Simon, advised the Home Office that the law should be restricted so that material 'intended in good faith to propagate opinion on religious subjects' should be prosecuted only if it were 'obscene or indecent'. But the Government did nothing, and further Bills failed to reach Second Readings in 1913 and 1914.

There was another brief lull at the beginning of the war, during which a literary work once again came under attack. Poetry had occasionally suffered from blasphemy prosecutions, perhaps because it is so quotable, but fiction had escaped — though Matthew Lewis's gothic romance *The Monk* (1796) had been threatened with prosecution for both obscene and blasphemous libel (it described the Bible as an immoral book), and an expurgated edition was quickly prepared with a new title, *Ambrosio, the Monk* (1798). In 1916 George Moore published *The Brook Kerith*, a novel based on the idea that Jesus survived the Crucifixion, renounced his messianic mission, and tried to dissuade Paul from his belief in the Resurrection. Lord Alfred Douglas attempted to bring a private prosecution for blasphemous libel, but he was refused a summons. (Douglas had a poor record with criminal libel: in 1895 he had incited Oscar Wilde to prosecute his father, the Marquess of Queensberry, for accusing him of homosexuality — the action which brought Wilde's ruin; in 1914 he was himself prosecuted for accusing Wilde's friend Robert Ross of homosexuality, but the jury disagreed; and in 1923 he was again prosecuted for accusing Winston Churchill of profiting from events in the First World War, and was imprisoned for six months.)

A civil case with an important bearing on the law of blasphemy lasted from 1914 to 1917. The will of Charles Bowman, leaving the residue of his estate to the Secular Society Limited (a company associated with the National Secular Society), was challenged by his family on several grounds, including the claim that the society's propaganda was blasphemous. The final judgement by the House of Lords included the statement that the phrase, 'Christianity is part of the law of England', repeated so often over two centuries, 'is really not law; it is rhetoric', and the recognition that the mere denial of Christianity or religion was not itself contrary to public policy. The main point of the case was that Freethought organisations could receive legacies without legal challenge, but an incidental point was the further secularisation of the law of blasphemy, which was stated to apply only to material which had a 'tendency to endanger the peace then and there, to deprave public morality generally, to shake the fabric of society, and to be a cause of civil strife', and which contained 'such an element of vilification, ridicule, or irreverence, as would be likely to exasperate the feelings of others and so lead to a breach of the peace'.

Nevertheless the wave of prosecutions against Secularist open-air speakers soon blew up again. Gott got two weeks in 1916 in Birkenhead and six weeks in 1917 in Birmingham; J. Riley got two weeks in 1917. There was another lull until the end of the war, and then the last two cases came in 1921, both involving Gott. In February he got three months in Birmingham, and in December he was arrested in Stratford, London, for obstruction but then faced his fifth and sixth trials for blasphemy (some of his cases involved contraceptive and anti-militarist as well as Secularist propaganda).

Gott was accused at the Central Criminal Court of distributing humorous publications with such titles as *God and Gott* and *Rib Ticklers: or Questions for Parsons* and annoying bystanders. His material was standard Freethought propaganda of a rather coarse kind, but no coarser than some Christian propaganda; indeed his *Questions for Parsons*, which caused so much offence, was a direct response to an Evangelical tract called *Questions for Infidels.* This brave if foolish man was arrested and tried and imprisoned over and over again until his death. At the end of 1921 the jury disagreed at the first trial, but at the second a new jury found him guilty, with a plea for clemency; on the contrary, after the police had described him as 'a socialist and atheist of the worst type', the judge gave him the savage sentence of nine months' hard labour.

The National Secular Society had long refused to have Gott as a member, but they supported him throughout the case and took it to the Court of Criminal Appeal in January 1922. The result was another authoritative ruling on the definition of the law of blasphemy (which was described by the Lord Chief Justice as 'a very dangerous crime') — that it covers material which is 'offensive to anyone in sympathy with the Christian religion, whether he be a strong Christian, or a lukewarm Christian, or merely a person sympathising with their ideas', who 'might be provoked to a breach of the peace'. One of the particular items for complaint in Gott's publications was the phrase that Jesus entered Jerusalem 'like a circus clown on the back of two donkeys'. As we have seen, this was a traditional item of Secularist propaganda, and though it may sound ridiculous it is based on a serious point of biblical criticism; one of the Evangelists misunderstands the Hebrew idiom of poetic parallelism in the Old Testament description of the King of Zion 'riding upon an ass, and upon a colt the foal of an ass' (*Zechariah* ix, 9), and taking it literally describes Jesus riding into Jerusalem on an ass and on her colt at the same time (*Matthew* xxi, 2-7). But such academic distinctions didn't apply to a man like Gott, who lost his appeal, served his sentence and, suffering from diabetes, died a few weeks after his release.

Gott was the last martyr of religious persecution in Britain, and his seems to have been the last blasphemy case for half a century. There were still occasional cases elsewhere in the British Empire — thus during the early 1930s there were prosecutions of C. L. d'Avoine in India, Victor Rahard in Canada, and Anne Lennon in Australia; and in 1940 A. R. Woodhall was sentenced to a month's imprisonment in Jersey for making a passport photograph resemble Christ on the Cross, but after protest he was released by the Home Secretary after a fortnight. Len Ebury, an open-air Secularist speaker in London, was fined in 1941, though not for blasphemy but under Hyde Park regulations, and he was threatened with the blasphemy law in 1958 but not prosecuted.

Gott's last case led to another lively controversy about the law. Courtney Kenny wrote an interesting article on its history in the *Cambridge Law Journal* (1922). Chapman Cohen, Foote's successor as editor of the *Freethinker* and president of the National Secular Society, who had organised Gott's defence, produced a widely circulated pamphlet, *Blasphemy: A Plea for Religious Equality* (1922). Bertrand Russell's Conway Memorial

Lecture, *Free Thought and Official Propaganda* (1922), which emphasised the surviving limitations on free thought, mentioned that 'in England, under the Blasphemy Laws, it is illegal to express disbelief in the Christian religion, though in practice the law is not set in motion against the well-to-do'; and a few years later his Secularist lecture, *Why I Am Not a Christian* (1927), proved the point by expressing powerful opposition to Christianity without being prosecuted.

In 1922 the Freethought organisations formed a new Society for the Abolition of the Blasphemy Laws, which carried on a vigorous campaign for several years. Unsuccessful attempts to introduce Bills into the House of Commons were made during the 1920s by J. F. Green, Harry Snell and George Lansbury. In 1929 a deputation saw the Labour Home Secretary, J. R. Clynes. In 1930 Ernest Thurtle (later secretary of the Rationalist Press Association) introduced a Blasphemy Laws (Amendment) Bill into the House of Commons, and it was actually given a Second Reading by a vote of 131 to 77, getting support from several progressive Christians as well as Freethinkers. But the Home Office was willing to kill it and the minority Labour Government was unwilling to save it, so the Catholic Solicitor General, James Melvill, introduced a wrecking amendment extending blasphemy to cover 'any matter of so scurrilous a character as to be calculated, by outraging the religious convictions of any other person, to provoke a breach of the peace', with a penalty of a £100 fine or a year's imprisonment. The Bill was withdrawn, and further attempts to introduce one during the 1930s failed.

After the Second World War the issue was almost forgotten, and occasional attempts to revive it got little support, even within the new Humanist movement. One senior judge, Lord Denning, in 1949 expressed the common view that 'the offence of blasphemy is a dead letter'; and another, Lord Goddard, referred in passing in 1951 to the 'somewhat obsolete offence of blasphemy'. In 1957 the Society for the Abolition of the Blasphemy Laws published R. S. W. Pollard's pamphlet *Abolish the Blasphemy Laws*, but in 1959 it was quietly dissolved. Yet in 1959 Ivor Jennings warned that the law of blasphemy was still 'so doubtful' that an intolerant court 'could make what it pleased of it'; and in 1964 Gerald Gardiner warned that 'there is no doubt that if the law relating to blasphemy were enforced in its full rigour, a stop could be put to much criticism and free thought'. During the period of law reform in the late 1960s the legal authorities took a hand by repealing all the obsolete old statutes, on the recommendation of the Law Commission in 1966; but a simultaneous recommendation by the Criminal Law Revision Committee that the common law offence should be abolished was ignored.

Meanwhile in the United States blasphemy remained a common law misdemeanour, and the various State laws were occasionally used but were generally restricted, repealed or found unconstitutional, until they survived in only half-a-dozen States; they were used very infrequently, and generally against extreme religious rather than anti-religious propagandists. In Scotland, as we have seen, the common law survives but seems to be in abeyance. In Ireland the Constitution, which established the Roman Cathoiic religion, specifically included blasphemy; but the English common law still applies, which could lead to characteristic anomalies if it were used. In the predominantly Christian White Dominions the various laws based on the English common law continue to exist, though they are virtually never used. In the other Dominions there are wider laws following the Indian model protecting all religions from direct insult likely to cause a breach of the peace.

Most countries have similar laws. In the Netherlands, Sweden, Norway and Denmark there are laws against such things as contempt of or insult to religion, though they are seldom used, and never with any success. In Italy and Austria there are similar laws, which have been used quite recently against militant anti-religious propaganda. In West Germany Section 166 of the Criminal Code protects 'the content of a religious or ideological (*weltanschaulich*) belief' and 'the institutions and practices of an established church or other religious society or ideological organisation (*Weltanschauungsvereinigung*)' from insult which is likely to disturb the public peace; no non-religious organisation ever seems to have invoked this unusual protection, which was introduced under the Weimar Republic, but the law has been used against militant anti-Christian propaganda on several occasions, until very recently, though without much success. In France and Belgium there is no law specifically protecting religion, but there is a provision deriving from the Napoleonic Code against offences contrary to 'public morality (*bonnes moeurs*)'.

In England and Wales the common law of blasphemy continued to exist in theory, but it seemed to have become obsolete in practice, like the common law of sedition. It remained in the law books, but that appeared to be where it belonged, and blasphemy like heresy was thought to have become a purely academic branch of English common law.

10 Permissiveness & Provocation

Blasphemy itself never ceased, in any sense. There was perhaps less of it in Freethought propaganda after Gott, because there was less need; but there was still plenty in ordinary usage and in serious art and literature.

At the time of Gott's last trial, a socialist paper in New Zealand, the *Maoriland Worker*, was prosecuted under the blasphemy law — but acquitted — for publishing Siegfried Sassoon's poem 'Stand-to: Good Friday Morning' (1916), which had appeared in two of his books, *The Old Huntsman* (1917) and *War Poems* (1918), and which ends as follows:

> O, Jesus, send me a wound to-day,
> And I'll believe in Your bread and wine,
> And get my bloody old sins washed white!

Rudyard Kipling had prefaced the first story, 'Lispeth', in his first collection, *Plain Tales From the Hills* (1888), with a poem called 'The Convert':

> Look, you have cast out Love! What Gods are these
>   You bid me please?
> The Three in One, the One in Three? Not so!
>   To my own gods I go.
> It may be they shall give me greater ease
> Than your cold Christ and tangled Trinities.

A. E. Housman included in his *Last Poems* (1922) a veiled defence of his veiled homosexuality which began as follows:

> The laws of God, the laws of man,
> He may keep that will and can;
> Not I: let God and man decree
> Laws for themselves and not for me;
> And if my ways are not as theirs
> Let them mind their own affairs.
> Their deeds I judge and much condemn,
> Yet when did I make laws for them? ...

W. B. Yeats included in his *Last Poems* (1939) a short squib called 'A Stick of Incense':

> Whence did all that fury come?
> From empty tomb or Virgin womb?
> Saint Joseph thought the world would melt,
> But liked the way his finger smelt.

Thomas Hardy published several poems as subversive as anything in Shelley or Swinburne, though not as offensive — especially 'God's Education' in *Time's Laughingstocks* (1909) and 'God's Funeral' in *Satires of Circumstance* (1914). T. S. Eliot's 'Hippopotamus' and W. H. Auden's 'Victor' have blasphemous implications, whatever their intentions. Several of D. H. Lawrence's 'Pansies' might have been condemned as blasphemous if so many hadn't been condemned as obscene.

Lawrence also produced a story which was remarkable both for its blasphemous content and its immunity from trouble. 'The Escaped Cock' was written in 1928, at the same time as *Lady Chatterley's Lover*, and published in the United States and France before appearing after his death in Britain as *The Man Who Died* (1931); it was later included in the second volume of his *Short Novels*. The story may be seen as a variation on the theme of *The Brook Kerith*, being based on the idea that Jesus survived the Crucifixion, met a priestess of Isis, and in making love with her experienced a true resurrection of the flesh similar to that in *Lady Chatterley's Lover*. The style is not as explicit as in the famous novel, but it is unequivocal in its identification of divine with sexual love.

E. M. Forster's story 'The Life to Come', which was written in 1922, was published only posthumously in 1972, but the delay was caused not so much by its blasphemous equation of divine and sexual love as by the fact that the love in question was homosexual.

James Joyce's novel *Ulysses* was first published in book form in France in 1922, but it was not freely available in Britain until 1936, after it had been found not to be obscene in the American trial of 1933 and appeal of 1934. Because of the long dispute about its obscenity, its blasphemy was overlooked, yet it is just as obvious. It begins with Buck Mulligan's grotesque parody of the Catholic Mass, and the opening episode also contains his 'Ballad of Joking Jesus':

I'm the queerest young fellow that ever you heard.
My mother's a Jew, my father's a bird.
With Joseph the joiner I cannot agree,
So here's to disciples and Calvary.

If anyone thinks that I amn't divine
He'll get no free drinks when I'm making the wine
But have to drink water and wish it were plain
That I make when the wine becomes water again.

Goodbye, now, goodbye. Write down all I said
And tell Tom, Dick and Harry I rose from the dead.
What's bred in the bone cannot fail me to fly,
And Olivet's breezy .... Goodbye, now, goodbye.

Bernard Shaw had trouble with the theatrical censorship over several of his plays, from *Mrs Warren's Profession* in 1894; and *The Shewing-up of Blanco Posnet*, which he described as 'a religious tract', was refused a licence by the Lord Chamberlain from 1909 to 1921 specifically because of its blasphemy (especially for such remarks about God as 'He's a sly one. He's a mean one'). Shaw used this experience for his attacks not only on theatrical censorship but on what he called 'the monstrous laws against blasphemy'. He also included several examples of blasphemy in his prefaces — especially those for *Androcles and the Lion* (1916) and *Back to Methuselah* (1921) — and in his story *The Adventures of the Black Girl in Search of God* (1932), which was as blasphemous as anything in the *Freethinker* half a century earlier.

On a rather different level, Marc Connelly's American play *The Green Pastures* (1929) was refused a licence in Britain in 1930, and the book was criticised but not prosecuted for its depiction of the God of the Old Testament as an overworked and bad-tempered Negro businessman. The rule seems to have been developed that blasphemy was acceptable on paper and even on the screen, but not on stage. Thus Michael Keighley's film of *The Green Pastures* (1936) was allowed in where the play was unable to tread. Several of the films of Luis Buñuel were as offensive as anything in old freethought propaganda, culminating in the parody of the Last Supper in *Viridiana* (1961); and Joseph Strick's film of *Ulysses* (1967) contained Joyce's blasphemous poem. Even in the theatre there was eventually a breeze of change, with the ludicrous arguments in 1958 whether Samuel Beckett could call God a 'bastard' or a 'swine' (because he doesn't exist) in the English version of *Endgame*. As a final irony, John Osborne's television play about Holyoake's trial in 1842, *A Subject of Scandal and Concern,* had difficulty getting broadcast in 1960.

Kingsley Amis included in *A Look Around the Estate* (1967) a poem called 'New Approach Needed':

> Should you revisit us,
> Stay a little longer,
> And get to know the place.
> Experience hunger,
> Madness, disease and war.
> You heard about them, true,
> The last time you came here;
> It's different having them ....
> On local life, we trust
> The resident witness,
> Not the royal tourist.
> People have suffered worse
> And more durable wrongs
> Than you did on that cross ....
> So, next time, come off it,
> And get some service in,
> Jack, long before you start
> Laying down the old law:
> If you still want to then.
> Tell your dad that from me.

Stevie Smith expressed similar sentiments at the same time in 'Was He Married?'; and she ended another poem, 'Thoughts about the Christian Doctrine of Eternal Hell', as follows:

> The religion of Christianity
> Is mixed of sweetness and cruelty.
> Reject this Sweetness, for she wears
> A smoky dress out of hell fires.
>
> Who makes a God? Who shows him thus?
> It is the Christian religion does.
> Oh, oh, have none of it,
> Blow it away, have done with it.
>
> This god the Christians show,
> Out with him, out with him, let him go.

Michael Moorcock wrote a science-fiction story called 'Behold the Man', which was first published in *New Worlds* in 1966 and later collected in *Moorcock's Book of Martyrs* (1978), in which a time-traveller goes back to see what really happened in first-century Palestine, finds that Jesus is an imbecile, and takes his place so that the Scriptures shall be fulfilled.

John Updike's novel *Marry Me* (1977) contained the following exchange:

'Heaven', Jerry said one night, entering her as she crouched above him. Afterward, he explained, 'I had this very clear vision of the Bodily Ascension, of me going up into this incredibly soft, warm, boundless sky: you.'

'Isn't that blasphemous?' ...

'Because it makes my prick Christ? I wonder. They both have this quality, of being more important than they should be. As Christ relates to the universe, my prick relates to me.'

'Then when I'm under you is that the descent into Hell?'

'No. You're Heaven in every direction ...'

Anthony Burgess's book *Abba Abba* (1977), a historical novel about Giuseppe Gioacchino Belli, the early nineteenth-century Italian poet, includes translations of more than seventy of Belli's blasphemous sonnets. One on the multiplicity of relics of Christ's foreskin goes as follows:

> That sacred relic, by the way, was hid
>   And either kept in camphor or else iced.
>   It grew so precious it could not be priced.
> And then one day His Holiness undid
> A holy box and raised a holy lid —
>   Behold — the foreskin of our saviour Christ,
>   Shrimplike in shape, most elegantly sliced,
> At last to profane eyes exhibited.
> In eighty other Christian lands they show
>   This self-same prize for reverent eyes to hail.
> You look incredulous, my friend. But know
>   That faith, though buffeted, must never fail.
> The explanation's this: God let it grow
>   After the clipping, like a fingernail.

At the same time religious and anti-religious controversy included much material which would once have been considered — and condemned — as blasphemy. John Robinson's *Honest to God* (1963) seemed to argue God out of any real existence in a way which offended many of his fellow Christians; and the symposium *The Myth of God Incarnate* (1977) seemed to argue against the divinity of Jesus in a way which was equally offensive. John Allegro's *The Sacred Mushroom and the Cross* (1970) claimed that Christianity began as a sex and drug cult based on the primitive worship of God as a penis in the sky and the ritual consumption of hallucinogenic mushrooms. Phyllis Graham's *The Jesus Hoax* (1974) claimed that not only the doctrine of Christianity but also the figure of Jesus are both intellectually and morally revolting.

All of this may have seemed shocking to some people, but it should be remembered that blasphemy in Britain has been remarkably mild compared to that elsewhere. In France, for example, it went much further much earlier, and has been a common element in avant-garde literature. The Marquis de Sade, who is well known for the extreme obscenity of his pornographic fantasies, is less well known for their extreme profanity. In his most objectionable novel, *Juliette* (1797), among all the sexual adventures there is a scene when a Cardinal recites an Ode describing universal sodomy among the Persons of the Trinity, the Virgin Mary and Mary Magdalene, and various angels, apostles and saints; this is expressed in such frank terms that the first open English translation, which was published in France and the United States in the 1960s, leaves it in French! The Comte de Lautréamont (Isidore Ducasse) included in his extraordinary fantasy *Maldoror* (1868-1869) repeated abuse of 'the Creator' not just traditionally as a tyrant and torturer but also as vermin, cannibal, drunkard, fornicator and homosexual, involving long passages of revolting obscenity; this has appeared in several English translations, including one in the Penguin Classics! And a favourite theme of the late nineteenth-century artist Félicien Rops was the obscene depiction of such sacred scenes as the Creation and the Fall, the Annunciation and the Crucifixion (the latter often involving Mary Magdalene or Teresa of Avila).

Back in Britain, the artist Eric Gill, who saw no distinction between the sacred and profane and who described his form of Catholicism as 'being fucked by Christ', often got into trouble for the explicitly sexual content of his religious drawings and carvings, though his work was censored rather than prosecuted. A good example is 'Nuptials of God' in the *Game* (January 1923), which explicitly depicts the Church as the naked Bride of the crucified Christ. Every now and then, however, there have been threats of and even attempts at prosecution for blasphemy. In 1953 Mark Boxer, editor of the student paper *Granta*, was expelled from Cambridge University for publishing a blasphemous poem by Anthony de Hoghton. Following the abolition of the Lord

Chamberlain's censorship of the theatre in 1968, several plays
were threatened (and in the case of *The Romans in Britain*
actually prosecuted) for obscenity, and there was also one attempt
at a prosecution for blasphemy. Oskar Panizza's play *The Council
of Love* had got him a year's imprisonment in Germany when it
was first published in Switzerland in 1894, and its theme is
certainly offensive enough — describing God asking the Devil to
infect mankind with syphilis as a punishment for the Vatican's
sins during the Renaissance! When it was performed in London
in 1970 (following a successful French production), the authorities
ignored complaints from the public, so the vigilantist leader Lady
Birdwood began a private prosecution of two directors (Jack Gold
and Eleanor Fazan); but in 1971 the case failed on technical
grounds, because the directors were not responsible for the
performance in question.

The modern vigilantist organisations, the Nationwide Festival
of Light and the National Viewers' and Listeners' Association, had
lost a battle, but they continued the campaign. In 1976 a new
element appeared, when Muslim interests successfully put
pressure on a Lebanese film about Muhammad, so that it could
be shown only if the prophet were not named in the title or shown
on the screen; it was eventually called *The Message* and had only
restricted circulation. On the other hand unorthodox depictions
of Jesus in such stage musicals as *Godspell* and *Jesus Christ
Superstar* or in such television plays as Dennis Potter's *Son of Man*
(1969), though they shocked some Christians, were untouched —
though transmission of the latter's equally unorthodox play about
the Devil, *Brimstone and Treacle* (1976), was delayed for several
years.

In a general climate of public opinion and expression which had
become so tolerant of extreme attacks on religion, the Danish film-
maker Jens Jorgen Thorsen tried to go one worse, and during the
mid-1970s there was an undignified public controversy about his
alleged plan for a film called *The Many Faces of Jesus* about the
supposed sex-life of Jesus, involving homosexual as well as
heterosexual activity. In 1976 the opposition to his proposal to
make the film in Britain reached a climax with protests from not
only the predictable vigilantist organisations but also the Queen,
the Prime Minister (James Callaghan) and the Archbishop of
Canterbury (Donald Coggan) — and the last two emphasised that
there was still a law of blasphemy to deal with such things. Also
in 1976, Louis Blom-Cooper and Gavin Drewry compiled *Law and
Morality,* an anthology on the relationship between the two; in

the introduction to the section on blasphemy they speculated prophetically: 'Perhaps this is one branch of the law which may still be sprung upon a hapless and unsuspecting defendant.'

The next step in the story of blasphemy law was taken by Mary Whitehouse, a leading vigilantist and the general secretary of NVALA, who was so fond of litigation against objectionable material that she was described as the Director of Private Prosecutions. She had often called for the revival of the blasphemy law — especially against the BBC for an episode of the television series *Till Death Us Do Part* in September 1972 — and at the end of 1976 she began a private prosecution against a poem which apparently described the supposed sex-life of Jesus. As has happened so often before, extreme 'permissiveness' turned into 'provocation', and the defenders of orthodoxy and decency struck back. Thus was the stage set for the *Gay News* case, and the apparently moribund law of blasphemy was brought back to life after more than half a century.

11 The *Gay News* Case

The two significant points about the *Gay News* case in the context of the long history of the blasphemy law are that it was the first which involved the element of homosexuality, and also the first which did not involve the element of an attack on Christianity.

The case concerned a serious work of literature by an established writer. James Kirkup was well known as a distinguished poet, novelist, dramatist, translator, broadcaster and critic. He had been a Fellow of the Royal Society of Literature since 1962, had taught English in universities all over the world, and had written poetry and drama expressing his interest in Christianity and his commitment to homosexuality. He lived in Japan, but still contributed to the British press. His poem 'The Love That Dares To Speak Its Name', which had been offered to several literary papers, was eventually published with an illustration by Tony Reeves in the homosexual fortnightly *Gay News* 96 (3/16 June 1976).

The title of the poem came from the last line of Lord Alfred Douglas's poem 'Two Loves', which had appeared in the first issue of *The Chameleon* in 1894, and which distinguished between heterosexual and homosexual love, the latter being called 'the love that dare not speak its name'. This poem played an important part in Oscar Wilde's first trial for homosexuality in 1895, when a prosecution question about the meaning of this line prompted Wilde's famous reply:

'The love that dare not speak its name' in this century is such a great affection of an elder for a younger man as there was between David and Jonathan, such as Plato made the very basis of his philosophy, and such as you find in the sonnets of Michelangelo and Shakespeare. It is that deep, spiritual affection that is pure as it is perfect. It dictates and pervades great works of art like those of Shakespeare and Michelangelo. It is in this century misunderstood, so much misunderstood that it may be described as 'the love that dare not speak its name'; and on account of it I am placed where I am now. It is beautiful, it is fine, it is the noblest form of affection. There is nothing unnatural about it. It is intellectual, and it repeatedly exists between an elder and a younger man, when the elder has intellect and the younger man has all the joy, hope and glamour of life before him. That it should be so, the world does not understand. The world mocks at it, and sometimes puts one in the pillory for it..

The point of Kirkup's poem is that in this century homosexual love has become, in the words of its last line, 'the love that now forever dares to speak its name'; and the theme of the poem was that it is a divine as well as a human love. So far so good, but the treatment was another matter. The 66-line poem and accompanying illustration expressed this theme in explicitly sexual terms, the fantasy being that the Roman centurion who pierced Christ's side on the Cross made love with his dying body afterwards, and the moral being that this union symbolises both a physical and a spiritual relationship between God and man.

Kirkup told the *New Humanist* that it was 'an old poem, part of a series of erotic works which I no longer wish to preserve' because 'it is not aesthetically a successful work' (November/December 1976). He later gave *Gay News* a statement about his reasons for writing the poem, but this could not be used in the trial because the judge ruled that literary evidence was inadmissible and the factor of intention irrelevant. (Extracts first appeared in the *Observer* on 17 July 1977.) Kirkup began by saying how he saw his own poem:

My poem in *Gay News*, like many of my religious poems, was an attempt to see Christ anew in terms of modern sexual liberation, terms valid for homosexuals, bisexuals and heterosexuals alike. I had always believed in Him as a real human being who had once lived on this earth, with lusts, failings, ecstasies and sexual equipment like the rest of us, and I was concerned to present this view with both humour and realism.

He went on to describe himself as 'a born unbeliever who yet longed to believe':

When I was a little boy, I suffered the misfortune of having to attend a Primitive Methodist Chapel and Sunday School. This dreadful place, like all Christian churches ever since, filled me with gloom, boredom, despondency and sheer terror. I heard the grisly, gory details of the Crucifixion for the first time at Sunday School at the age of five. I was so overcome by revulsion and fright that I fainted with the shock of those gruesome, violent images. When I heard of the fires of Hell and the torments of the damned, my horror expressed itself in outbursts of uncontrollable giggles, my knees shook, and I wet the floor. I, who loathed meat and could not even bear the sight of a cut finger, was informed that I could be 'saved' only if I were to be washed in the Blood of the Lamb — which my poor dear parents considered a Sunday lunchtime luxury. I could never take part in Holy Communion, for the very thought of eating bits of Christ's dead flesh and drinking cups of his blood made me sick.

Now I am convinced that young people with impressionable minds should never be exposed to such brutal, sadistic and violent obscenities, whether in church, in books, in the cinema or on television. I wonder how many children were utterly disgusted by Christianity as I was through the constant repetititon of these inartistic, tasteless and crude images.

So I was never a Christian, though I often felt I ought to be. I liked the legends and the character of Christ Jesus. To me He was the friend I never found in real life, for I was a solitary right from the start.

Hence the desperate appeal of his poem:

My poem was to be all things to all men. It was to express passionate love of Christ, with intense realism. The 'love that dares to speak its name' of my title is not specifically homosexual love, but simply and purely the passionate love of a great and exceptional individual rejected and murdered by conventional society. This is the kind of love the Church does not allow us to think about, and which most people fail to imagine in the banal religiosity of worship. The poem reflects my deeply religious nature. It is about the mystery of miracles — the miracles of the conversion of the centurion Longinus, and the resurrection of the dead body of Jesus through our human, earthly loves and desires. I wanted to portray strong, deep emotion and intense passion (in both senses of the word), to present a human, earthly and imperfect Christ symbolising my own outcast state, and that of all outcasts in our society.

Of course I knew this would dismay and shock some people — but had I not myself been deeply offended, dismayed and shocked by their disgusting version of the Crucifixion? As for blasphemy — that was never my intention. How could it be? It never entered my head for one moment that the poem might be misconstrued in that way. My motives were pure — on that my conscience is clear — and all I wanted was to create a work of art. Audacity yes, blasphemy no.

When the poem was published in *Gay News*, there was some critical correspondence in subsequent issues, but eventually this came to an end, and it fell into the obscurity which is the usual fate of publication in a minority periodical. In the normal course of events it would have been quietly included in a future collection of Kirkup's poems. On this occasion, however, its obscurity was to be disturbed and normality to be interrupted. Kenneth Kavanagh, a Bedford probation officer, later said that he bought a copy of the issue in question because he wanted to read its front-page report of the Annual Conference of the National Association of Probation Officers, that three months later he noticed the poem on page 26, and that he then complained to a fellow member of the Responsible Society. (The controversy over the Thorsen film reached its climax in September 1976, which suggests a chronological as well as ideological connection between the two cases.) What happened next remains uncertain, but it is clear that there was frantic activity among the various vigilantist organisations and that the legal, political and religious authorities refused to take any action. In November 1976 Mary Whitehouse announced that she would begin a private prosecution for blasphemous libel against *Gay News*, its editor Denis Lemon, and its distributors.

In December a judge gave permission for the prosecution to proceed, which is necessary in the case of newspapers, and granted a voluntary bill of indictment, which enabled the case to go to trial without committal proceedings in a magistrates court; and the case against the distributors was dropped. During the next six months *Gay News* raised £20,000 in donations — about £1 per purchaser — to pay for its defence, and both sides prepared their cases. Meanwhile the prosecution had as usual revived interest in the offending article. *Gay News* 96 became a precious collectors' item, and the poem was soon being widely circulated. From December 1976 it was reprinted as a duplicated leaflet by the Free Speech Movement, and from the beginning of 1977 it was reprinted in several left-wing papers — the Young Liberal

Liberator in January, the pacifist *Peace News* on 28 January, the
Anarchist Worker in February/March, the Trotskyist *Socialist
Challenge* on 14 July, the anarchist *Freedom* on 23 July, and in
several local community and student papers.

Everyone concerned with the conduct of the prosecution and
the trial repeatedly denied that the *Gay News* case had anything
to do with the fact that the poem and the paper were homosexual,
but there is little doubt that this was a very important element,
and there is much doubt whether a similarly explicit heterosexual
poem about Jesus in a literary or political paper would have
suffered the same fate. Everyone concerned with the defence
repeatedly denied that the poem was written or published as an
attack on Christianity, and there is little doubt that this was not
the intention of either the author or the editor, however much
it may have been carelessly misunderstood by some of its readers
and was deliberately misconstrued by its persecutors.

★ ★ ★

The trial of Denis Lemon and *Gay News* was held in the Central
Criminal Court in London in July 1977 (see *New Humanist*,
May/August 1977). The judge was Alan King-Hamilton, a
prominent figure in the Reform Jewish community, who was well
known as an eccentric and outspoken occupant of the Bench with
strong traditionalist views, and who was obviously sympathetic
to the prosecution throughout the trial. The prosecuting counsel
was John Smyth, a young barrister with a military manner who
was unwisely underestimated by the defence. The defence
counsel for Denis Lemon was John Mortimer, the well-known left-
wing barrister and writer, and for *Gay News* Geoffrey Robertson,
a young left-wing barrister and journalist.

The indictment described the offending publication as 'a
blasphemous libel concerning the Christian religion, namely an
obscene poem and illustration vilifying Christ in his life and in
his crucifixion'. The defence began by challenging the indictment
on several grounds, all of which were rejected by the judge. The
defence then challenged the maximum number of jurors without
cause — seven for each defendant — in an attempt to exclude the
more obviously uneducated or conventional. All twelve eventually
chosen — including five women and two Black men — took the
Christian oath.

Because of the great uncertainty about the common law of
blasphemy, most of the hearing was taken up with legal arguments
in the absence of the jury. The defence made a long series of

submissions — that the common law offence of blasphemy no longer existed, because of the long period of disuse and because of changes in both English and international law; that, even if it did still exist, it had changed in the half-century since it was last invoked; that expert witnesses should be called to give evidence on religious and literary matters; that there was no evidence that Denis Lemon was responsible for the publication of the poem; that the prosecution must prove the intent to blaspheme and the tendency to cause a breach of the peace. The judge rejected each one in turn.

The prosecution case was very short and very simple. It proved that the poem had been published by *Gay News* under the editorship of Denis Lemon, that a copy of the issue in question had been bought by Kenneth Kavanagh, and that he had been shocked and angered by it. It took the poem as a literal attack on Christianity, describing it as being 'so vile it would be hard for the most perverted imagination to conjure up anything worse', and rejecting any suggestion that it was obviously intended to be a fantastic and imaginative work of art rather than a programmatic or polemical work of criticism.

The defence case was also very short because most of its submissions were rejected by the judge, but it was far from simple. In the absence of expert witnesses, the journalist Bernard Levin and the novelist and critic Margaret Drabble were called as witnesses to the character of *Gay News*; both made brave and generous efforts to do their best for the paper, but mainly showed how little they were aware of its explicitly sexual character. The long closing speeches by both defence counsel emphasised the literary aspects of the poem, seen as an unorthodox religious work rather than an anti-religious one.

The judge summed up strongly against the defence, insisting that it was a simple case and a simple poem. He defined blasphemy as anything concerning God, Christ, or the Christian religion in terms so scurrilous, abusive or offensive as to outrage the feelings of any member of or sympathiser with the Christian religion and to tend to lead to a breach of the peace. He excluded the element of intent, except so far as it applied to the intent to publish the writing. He hinted that the law might cover religions other than Christianity (a point which he repeated in his Winston Churchill Lecture in February 1979). And he referred to the poem in terms of personal disgust as 'the ultimate in profanity'.

The jury considered their verdict for five hours, were unable to reach a unanimous verdict, and eventually returned majority verdicts of 10 to 2 that both *Gay News* and Denis Lemon were guilty of publishing a blasphemous libel. The judge sentenced Denis Lemon to nine months' imprisonment (suspended for eighteen months) and a fine of £500, sentenced *Gay News* to a fine of £1,000, and also awarded the prosecution costs against them.

The appeal against both conviction and sentence was heard in the Criminal Division of the Court of Appeal in February 1978, and judgement was given in March 1978 (see *New Humanist*, Spring 1978); the three Appeal Judges unanimously upheld the conviction, though they quashed the prison sentence on Denis Lemon. The final appeal to the House of Lords was heard in November 1978 (John Mortimer being replaced as leading defence counsel by Louis Blom-Cooper), and judgement was given in February 1979 (see *New Humanist*, March 1979); the five Law Lords by a majority of three to two dismissed the appeal.

There were many grounds of appeal, but the main issues considered both in the Appeal Court and in the House of Lords were those of the intent of the publisher of an alleged blasphemous libel and of the tendency of such publication to cause a breach of the peace. The appellants argued that there must be an element of an attack on the Christian religion in the offending item, and of an intention in the defendant to make such an attack; and also that there must be some genuine likelihood of an actual breach of the peace resulting from the offending item. None of the Appeal Judges or Law Lords showed any interest in the element of a tendency to a breach of the peace, but the two minority Law Lords — Lord Diplock and Lord Edmund-Davies — both took a 'milder view of the law' in the tradition of Coleridge a century earlier, and agreed that the element of subjective intention should be admissible, at least to the extent that a defendant should be able to raise a doubt about it. This would certainly have been important in this case, since neither the author of the poem nor the editor of *Gay News* had intended to attack Christianity. But all the Appeal Judges and the three majority Law Lords agreed that the only element of intent which was relevant was that of publishing an item which was found blasphemous.

All the Appeal Judges and Law Lords accepted King-Hamilton's definition of blasphemy; and one of the Law Lords — Lord Scarman — in the last passage of the last judgement in the last hearing in the case revived the old definition in the 1950 edition of James Fitzjames Stephen's *Digest of the Criminal Law*: a blasphemy is 'any contemptuous, reviling, scurrilous or ludicrous matter relating to God, Jesus Christ, or the Bible, or the formularies of the Church of England'; but 'it is not blasphemous to speak or publish opinions hostile to the Christian religion, or to deny the existence of God, if the publication is couched in decent and temperate language'; so 'the test to be applied is as to the manner in which the doctrines are advocated and not as to the substance of the doctrines themselves'. Lord Scarman also argued that the blasphemy law should be extended to protect all religions, and that such a provision was implicit in the *Universal Declaration of Human Rights* and in the *European Convention on Human Rights.*

Gay News appealed to the European Court of Human Rights, but in May 1982 the European Commission of Human Rights decided that the case was inadmissible. This marked the end of the legal battle.

★   ★   ★

One ironical aspect of the *Gay News* case was that human justice was apparently insufficient to ensure the correct result, for both the prosecution and the judge invoked divine intervention. Mary Whitehouse conducted prayers outside the court during the trial, and according to her biography — *Whitehouse* (1979) by Michael Tracey and David Morrison — she afterwards claimed the presence of the 'Holy Spirit' inside it. Alan King-Hamilton said in his autobiography *And Nothing But The Truth* (1983) that in his conduct of the trial 'I was half-conscious of being guided by some superhuman inspiration'. The theology of blasphemy cases is a subject that would clearly repay investigation.

The historical result of the case was that Mary Whitehouse had made the first successful use of the blasphemy law since 1921, its first successful use against the press since 1883, and its first successful use against a serious work of literature since 1841.

The legal result was that the law of blasphemy was not (as most people had come to assume) either an ultimate safeguard whose retention was necessary for extreme cases, or a dead letter whose repeal was unnecessary because it was obsolete, but (as Freethinkers had always argued) a living threat to freedom of expression in religious matters. Moreover, it not only continued to exist but was as strong as ever, if not more so. Its basic definition was not changed, but the elements of a 'guilty mind' (*mens rea*) — the intention of the defendant to attack Christianity — and of the tendency of item to cause a breach of the peace, both of which had been taken for granted in the past, were reduced to virtually nothing, and blasphemy had become an offence of almost 'strict liability' to which virtually no defence was possible. According to J. R. Spencer, the absurd result seems to be that 'it is now a blasphemous libel to publish words attacking or ridiculing the Christian religion which might possibly make believers angry' (*Cambridge Law Journal*, November 1979); indeed the willingness of a single person to start a prosecution would presumably be sufficient evidence to secure a conviction.

There were times during the various hearings, as judges quoted judges quoting judges going back over a period of more than three centuries, when the real world seemed to have been forgotten altogether, and it often seemed that the whole immensely expensive process was designed to keep many otherwise intelligent men in gainful employment and to fill the lawbooks with material which — unlike the poem at the centre of it all — no one would ever want to read again. In the end the rational reaction to the case echoed that of Mr Bumble: 'If the law supposes that', he says of a similar legal nonsense in Charles Dickens' *Oliver Twist*, 'the law is a ass — a idiot.' (This is written from the perspective of the only outsider who attended all the hearings.)

The main practical result of the case, however, was the enormous circulation of the poem in question far beyond its original readership in a relatively obscure paper. Although no serious papers dared to reprint it and several libraries refused to issue it, it continued to be reprinted in minority papers and distributed in leaflet editions, and it was sometimes read out at public meetings and debates. The Free Speech Movement continued to circulate copies, and in February 1978 issued a special leaflet edition signed by more than a hundred prominent people.*

Other results were a strong reinforcement of the campaign for gay liberation, and a mutual recognition of the place of Humanism in the homosexual movement and of homosexuals in the Humanist movement. There was a large protest demonstration in central London on 11 February 1978. Mary Whitehouse had frequently referred to a 'humanist homosexual lobby', although none existed, but her action led to one; in 1979 the Gay Humanist Group was

---

* A later leaflet edition of 'The Love That Dares To Speak its Name' is still available on request and receipt of a stamped addressed envelope from the Free Speech Movement, 84B Whitechapel High Street, London E1.

formed, and as the Gay and Lesbian Humanist Association it
became one of the liveliest sections of the Freethought movement.
  There was widespread discussion of the case and of the
blasphemy law in the media; expert legal comment was
overwhelmingly hostile to the decisions of the Appeal Court and
the House of Lords. One of the most intelligent comments on the
case came in *Buddhism and Blasphemy* (1979), a pamphlet
written by Maha Sthavira Sankharakshita (formerly D. P. E.
Lingwood) and published by the Western Buddhists, which
contained a well-written and well-argued attack on the law and
concept of blasphemy and also on Christianity. Several books on
the case were planned, but none was written, and no full account
has been published. A useful documentary record was supplied
by a television reconstruction of the trial, together with several
interviews, which was broadcast in the BBC *Everyman* series on
18 September 1977 and again on 26 February 1978; and a follow-
up programme was broadcast after the first appeal on 19 March
1978.
  Immediately after the trial, in August 1977, a Committee Against
Blasphemy Law was formed by representatives of the national
Freethought organisations, on the initiative of William McIlroy,
the retiring secretary of the National Secular Society (who was
convicted the following month of sending copies of the poem
through the post, though for indecency rather than blasphemy).
It issued a founding Manifesto in September 1977 (see *New
Humanist*, September/October 1977) and a Statement Against
Blasphemy Law signed by well over a hundred prominent people
in January 1978 (see *New Humanist*, January/February 1978), and
it launched a Petition Against Blasphemy Law (see *New Humanist*,
Spring 1978).
  This campaign obtained impressive support, but it achieved no
success. In February 1978 Lord Willis (the writer Ted Willis)
introduced a Bill to abolish the blasphemy law into the House of
Lords, but it was withdrawn after a hostile debate on the Second
Reading, in which several speakers favoured the extension rather
than the abolition of the law (see *New Humanist*, Spring 1978).
In 1979 the *Report on Obscenity and Film Censorship* by the
Bernard Williams Committee recommended the abolition of the
offence of blasphemy as well as of obscenity, but all its
recommendations were ignored.
  A later attempt to reform the law of blasphemy was made by
the legal authorities. The Law Commission issued a Working Paper
in April 1981 and a final report in June 1985 on *Offences against*

Religion and Public Worship. The former, after considering the history and employment of the law, made the provisional recommendation that on balance 'the common law offences of blasphemy and blasphemous libel should be abolished and that there should be no statutory replacement'. The latter, after considering the various comments received, included two recommendations: the majority repeated the recommendation that the common law offences should be abolished 'without replacement'; the minority made the recommendation that the common law should be abolished but replaced by a statute law against 'grossly abusive or insulting material relating to a religion with the purpose of outraging religious feelings' (which would extend the theoretical coverage of the law, though it would reintroduce the element of intent and make convictions very difficult), and at the same time added that prosecutions would have to be approved by the Director of Public Prosecutions (which would restrict its practical application to vanishing-point). But all these recommendations were ignored.

The *Gay News* case was accompanied and followed by some amusing events. At the time of the trial itself, in 1977, John Mortimer had a play on in London called *The Bells of Hell*, a farce about an atheist bishop, a modernist vicar, and a traditionalist curate who turned out to be the Devil. In 1976 G. W. Target had published a novel called *The Triumph of Vice* in which a novel describing the love of Jesus Christ and Mary Magdalene is condemned (though not prosecuted) by Christian vigilantists for its sensational treatment of the sexual theme. In 1977 Barbara Smoker, the president of the National Secular Society, produced *Good God!*, a collection of satirical poems which were as blasphemous in the strict sense as anything by James Kirkup. Anthony Burgess later included in his novel *Earthly Powers* (1980) the trial for blasphemy of a homosexual poem, 'The Love Songs of J. Christ by Valentine Wrigley'; several technical details are wrong (the case is started by a public prosecution, is heard in a magistrates court, is not so much a trial as an inquiry, and expert evidence is allowed), but the arguments closely parallel the *Gay News* case.

More serious examples of blasphemy soon appeared. The film of *Monty Python's Life of Brian* (1979), a hilarious satire on the life and death of Jesus, caused widespread controversy but was widely shown with complete impunity; so was Jean-Luc Godard's *Hail Mary!* (1984), a modernised and secularised view of the Annunciation; and Martin Scorsese's film of Nikos Kazantzakis's

novel *The Last Temptation of Christ* (1988), which explored the
sexual nature of Jesus, caused even more anger but was also
widely shown with impunity from prosecution though not from
protest (especially in the United States). Michele Roberts's novel
The Wild Girl (1984) caused protests, including a threat of
prosecution for blasphemy, for its feminist account of a Gospel
by Mary Magdalene describing her relations (including sexual
relations) with Jesus.

In 1989 the blasphemy law was invoked again, though this time
in connection with the provisions of the Video Recording Act of
1984. *Visions of Ecstasy*, Nigel Wingrove's short video film about
Teresa of Avila, which linked her mystical experiences with
explicitly sexual treatment of the dead body of Jesus, was refused
a certificate by the British Board of Film Classification in
September and lost its appeal to the Video Appeals Committee
in December on the ground that it was blasphemous (see *New
Humanist*, January 1990). The two-day appeal hearing was
strongly reminiscent of the *Gay News* trial and appeals twelve
years before — though a new element was expert evidence by
literary and religious witnesses (Nicholas Cooke, Colin MacCabe,
Sara Maitland, Marina Warner, Fay Weldon). The case had the
same sense of complete unreality, as the lawyers — Richard Du
Cann for the censors and Geoffrey Robertson for the producers
— debated the precise degree of sexuality attributed to Jesus; and
this sense was reinforced when the Video Appeals Committee
issued the text of its decision in January 1990.

By this time, however, a much more dramatic new chapter in
the story of blasphemy had been opened by Salman Rushdie's
novel *The Satanic Verses.*

12 The *Satanic Verses* Case

The *Satanic Verses* case again concerned a serious work of
literature by an established writer. Salman Rushdie (an anglicised
form of Rashdi) came from a Muslim Indian family and was born
in Bombay in 1947, but he was educated in England and settled
in London. He lost his faith, and said that he had 'a God-shaped
hole' which he tried to fill with literature. He became a member
of the British literary establishment — the author of several very
successful novels, especially *Midnight's Children* (1981) and
Shame (1983), a Fellow of the Royal Society of Literature, and
a leading figure in the British Film Institute and the Institute of
Contemporary Arts. He also became a member of the left-wing
intelligentsia — well-known for a television talk in the Channel
Four *Opinions* series, in which he said that Britain is a hopelessly
racist and imperialist country ('The New Empire Within Britain',
New Society, 9 December 1982).

His novel *The Satanic Verses* was published in London in
September 1988, and won the Whitbread Prize for fiction in
November 1988. It is an extraordinary fantasy covering many
topics — emigration and immigration, India and Britain, Islam and
Christianity, good and evil, angels and devils, blacks and whites,
males and females, belief and unbelief, truth and falsehood. There
is a bitter caricature of life in contemporary Britain, in which the
Prime Minister appears as 'Mrs Torture' and 'Maggie the Bitch',
policemen, prison officers and immigration officials appear as
sadistic thugs, and racism appears as the main feature of the land.
This aroused comment but not condemnation; what led to real
trouble was the treatment of Islam.

In two sections of the book — involving 76 out of 550 pages —
there is a dream sequence about the foundation of Islam. This part
of the book — and indeed the whole book, as reflected in its title
— revolves around the traditional story that, when Muhammad
composed the *Koran* on the dictation of the Archangel Gabriel,
Satan tried to insert some verses (in Sura 53) which accepted three
of the old goddesses of the Arabs. Other themes in this part of
the book are that Muhammad behaved as a calculating politician
rather than an inspired prophet, that he composed the *Koran* and
made laws with practical rather than religious motives, and that
his sex life was disreputable. He is called 'Mahound' (the old

Christian term of abuse), and there are many other words and phrases and ideas which are offensive to orthodox Muslims. The book also contains attacks on 'the Imam', who is obviously the Ayatollah Ruhollah Khomeini, a leading figure in the Shi'a sect and the spiritual power behind the revolutionary regime in Iran.

Rushdie himself said, 'I have tried to give a secular, humanist vision of the birth of a new religion', though he added that *The Satanic Verses* is not ... an anti-religious novel' (*Observer*, 22 January 1989); and he also said, 'One of the main impetuses behind the book was to make some kind of secular confrontation with the idea of revelation' (*Bookseller*, 31 March 1989). He was certainly aware of its blasphemous connotations. He gives his own name to Mahound's secretary, who is caught falsifying texts of the *Koran* and is told — all too prophetically: 'Your blasphemy, Salman, can't be forgiven. Did you think I wouldn't work it out? To set your words against the Words of God.' Salman's life is saved — let us hope also prophetically.

The trouble is that such a theme, which has become more or less acceptable in Christian or post-Christian culture, is not yet acceptable in Muslim culture. Rationalism and scepticism have existed in the Muslim world almost from the beginning, and have affected some of its greatest figures — such as al-Ghazzali, Omar Khayyam, and Ibn Rushd (Averroes) — but they have normally been suppressed as severely as they used to be in the Christian world. In Muslim countries today sceptical writers — including some of the greatest, such as the Egyptian Nobel Prize-winner Nagib Mahfuz — are frequently censored. Muslim culture, with this traditional attitude to unorthodoxy, has followed Asian immigration into many non-Muslim countries, including Britain, and the resulting culture clash has caused increasing problems. During the 1970s and 1980s militant Muslims in Western countries had attempted to suppress various kinds of material which were offensive to them as followers of Islam rather than as members of minority races, and such groups began a campaign against *The Satanic Verses* in October 1988.

It must be emphasised that the trouble was started not by the publication of the book but by the campaign against it. The book was published in a completely normal way, with no suggestion of an attack on the Muslim community, and there is no evidence that any casual reader was disturbed by it. The campaign against the book, which was begun by Muslim politicians in India and imported into Britain by the Islamic Foundation in Leicester, involved the deliberate incitement of anger among Muslims who

would otherwise not have read or even heard of the book. This
was done through the widespread distribution of relevant extracts
by a few militant leaders among a very large number of
organisations and then individuals, in Britain and around the
world, enormously increasing the circulation of the allegedly
offensive passages, together with demands for protests and
actions against the book. This campaign led to the book being
banned in November 1988 by India and Pakistan (whose rulers
had been insulted by *Midnight's Children* and *Shame*
respectively), South Africa, and most Muslim countries.

The national campaign was unsuccessful in that it was ignored
by the publishers and also the authorities in Britain, so from
December 1988 the Muslim militants began to seek publicity by
organising demonstrations in several provincial towns and then
in London, involving the public burning of copies of the book and
occasional riots, and leading to the withdrawal of the book from
some shops. The international campaign was more successful, and
reached a climax on 14 February 1989, when Ayatollah Khomeini
delivered a *fatwa* (religious judgement) that Salman Rushdie
should be killed for his blasphemy. This sort of action, which
seems quite outrageous nowadays, was once quite common.
Religious leaders, like political leaders, used to have their
opponents assassinated as a matter of course. In the Christian
world the Pope excommunicated and outlawed Queen Elizabeth
in 1570, and Mormon leaders are still having their rivals murdered;
in the Muslim world Muhammad's successors resorted to
assassination within a few years of his death, and the very word
assassin comes from a murderous Shi'a sect founded in eleventh-
century Iran. Khomeini had frequently used the old weapon
against his Iranian opponents, but his introduction of it into the
Satanic Verses case made it a global issue.

Rushdie quickly issued a statement regretting that his book had
caused distress to Muslims, but the campaigns continued and led
not only to riots in which several people were killed but to an
international crisis. Diplomatic relations between Iran and most
Western countries were broken during March. Also in March the
international Islamic Conference Organisation condemned the
book, though it didn't endorse the death sentence. However it
was echoed by Muslim leaders in many countries — including
Britain, where it was repeated many times both in spoken words
and in writing, without any legal action against anyone. Rushdie
was forced to go into hiding under police protection; there were
threats and even attacks on the staff and premises of several

publishers and booksellers; there were also large demonstrations and occasional riots in several places. Khomeini died in June 1989, but the death sentence remained in force.

One interesting point was that official spokesmen for the Church of England, the Roman Catholics and the Orthodox Jews agreed that the book was blasphemous, though they didn't endorse the death sentence either. Another was that Muslims in Italy threatened to attack the Dante memorial in Ravenna, in a rather belated reaction to *The Divine Comedy*.

The literary establishment and the civil liberties movement responded more slowly in Britain than elsewhere, but eventually reacted strongly against the campaign. Article 19, the British section of an international civil liberties organisation, formed an International Committee for the Defence of Salman Rushdie and His Publishers, which mustered support from all over the world; it prepared a *World Statement* on the subject which was issued in March 1989 with several hundred signatures and reissued in July 1989 with several thousand signatures, and it published a pamphlet on *The Crime of Blasphemy: Why it Should be Abolished* in May 1989. A public reading of passages from *The Satanic Verses* was initiated by Larry Adler and organised by the South Place Ethical Society at Conway Hall in London on 2 July 1989.

There was widespread discussion of the case in the media. A few of the contributions have had more permanent value — a special issue of *Index on Censorship* on Islam and Human Rights (May/June 1989), Fay Weldon's CounterBlasts pamphlet *Sacred Cows* (July 1989), the documentary collection by Sarah Maitland and Lisa Appignanesi called *The Rushdie File* (July 1989), Timothy Brennan's book *Salman Rushdie and the Third World* (September 1989), Rana Kabbani's booklet *Letter to Christendom* (October 1989), and Malise Ruthven's book *The Satanic Affair* (February 1990). The controversy also stimulated some literary works. *Iranian Nights*, a satirical play by Howard Brenton and Tariq Ali, had a short run in London in April 1989; and *The Blasphemers' Banquet*, a television fantasy in verse by Tony Harrison which associated Rushdie with Omar Khayyam, Molière, Voltaire and Byron, was broadcast by the BBC in July 1989.

The main effect of the case was increased polarisation between the Asian community and the rest of society, and between religious fundamentalism and political secularism within the Asian community. Just as the *Gay News* case had raised the profile of Humanism within the homosexual community, the *Satanic Verses* case raised the profile of secularism within the Asian Community.

This was expressed in May 1989 by the appearance of some interesting new organisations. Voices for Salman Rushdie, formed by a coalition of socialist, feminist and anti-racist groups and individuals in London, voiced solidarity with Rushdie personally, but also protested against the racist undertones of the controversy and the tendency to identify the whole Asian community with the fanatical leaders, and advocated a programme including such secularist demands as the abolition of the blasphemy law and of state-funded denominational schools. And Women Against Fundamentalism, an offshoot of the same coalition, made much the same demands with particular emphasis on the position of women in religious communities.

From the perspective of the blasphemy law, the main point of the case was the militant Muslim demand that *The Satanic Verses* should be banned as a blasphemous libel. Since the Government was unable to do this by executive action and unwilling to begin legal action, the only course would have to be a private prosecution of the publishers. But for this to have any prospect of success there would have to be either a decision by a court that the common law covers Islam or else a new Act of Parliament amending the common law to cover Islam. In March 1989 the Action Committee for Islamic Affairs was refused a summons for a private prosecution, but in April 1989 it was granted a judicial review to consider the former question; meanwhile several organisations also demanded the latter action, but this was rejected by the Government in February and again in July 1989.

The discussion of this issue was affected by the strong political implications of the case. The Labour Party has traditionally been more concerned than other major parties with the welfare of immigrant communities, most Muslims (and other Asians) in Britain have traditionally voted Labour, and several Labour constituencies are dominated by Asian voters. As a result some Labour politicians, including a few Members of Parliament, argued that the blasphemy law should be extended to cover the religions followed by Asian communities. On the other hand the Labour Party has always been more concerned than other major parties with freedom of expression. As a result, several other Labour politicians, including some leading Members of Parliament, argued that the blasphemy law should be abolished, partly to end the discrimination between Anglican Christianity and other religions, and partly to end the discrimination between religious and other beliefs. At the other end of the political spectrum, some of the

right-wing opposition to the Muslim protests against the book and
demands for legal action had distinctly racist overtones.

The Humanist movement reacted strongly to the Rushdie case.
The various national and international organisations opposed the
campaign against *The Satanic Verses* and the demand for the
extension of the blasphemy law, and protested against the death
sentence. Two leading members — Barbara Smoker of the National
Secular Society and Nicolas Walter of the Rationalist Press
Association — held a counter-demonstration during the huge
London demonstration organised by the Muslim Action Front on
27 May 1989 with banners calling for Free Speech, and were
physically attacked though not seriously hurt by the mob. The case
clearly raised important issues about the place of fanatical religion
in a pluralist society which have always been primary concerns
of the Freethought movement.

13 The Blasphemy Law

The history of blasphemy cases — and of heresy cases before them
— inevitably concentrates on the peaks of religious persecution;
below the surface religious prejudice has always been more
pervasive and persuasive than may appear from these occasional
and ineffective prosecutions, and it remains powerful and
dangerous — as has emerged from recent events. In our pluralist
society, where many forms of Christianity have been joined by
many other forms of religion, and where at least half the
population never voluntarily attend any religious ceremony and
at least a quarter have no religious belief, legal protection for the
enforcement of religious prejudice seems an anachronistic and
absurd survival of past oppression.

The controversy about *The Satanic Verses* and then about
Visions of Ecstasy led to a renewal of the controversy about
blasphemy law. The Committee Against Blasphemy Law was
revived in February 1989. In May 1989 it issued a Statement
Against Blasphemy Law signed by more than 200 prominent
people (see *New Humanist*, June 1989), and it encouraged various
attempts to abolish the law. In April 1989 Tony Benn introduced
a Bill to that effect into the House of Commons, exactly a century
after Charles Bradlaugh had first done so; but it fell without
debate.

The position taken by the Committee, expressing the views of
the Humanist movement, is that there are four possible ways of
dealing with the present law of blasphemy, as follows.

Inaction

The easiest thing is always to follow Lord Melbourne's advice,
'When in doubt what to do, do nothing'; and the easiest thing to
do with the blasphemy law is nothing — leave the common law
as it is, with all its uncertainty and unpredictability, on the
grounds that it acts as a sort of Government Health Warning about
going too far in religious controversy, is never used by the
authorities and seldom by anyone else, and is part of our rich
national heritage of old-fashioned muddle.

This is the position of the Government, of the Home Office, of
many Conservatives, and probably of most people in power —
though of only 7 per cent of the population (according to a survey
by Public Attitude Surveys in October 1989). The obvious
advantage is that no one has to take any time or trouble doing
anything; the obvious disadvantage is that the present law is
uncertain and unrestricted, and that it could easily be used again
against serious controversy or art. The one thing which was clear
in the *Gay News* case was that the present situation is
unsatisfactory.

An alternative approach would be to follow the general trend
away from common law to statute law, and to formalise the
existing provisions by codifying the offence in an Act of
Parliament, following the wording of Stephen's *Digest of the
Criminal Law*, amended in the light of the decisions in the *Gay
News* case. The advantages are that this would at least make the
situation simpler and would make any future trials shorter. The
disadvantages are that such an action would tend to formalise a
bad law and would lead to wider discussion of the law and to
various proposals for amendment, in one of two obvious
directions, as follows.

Extension

If anything is to be done about the present law, the second easiest
thing to do is to widen it beyond Anglican Christianity, so as to
remove the discrimination against the large number of people in
the country who follow other forms of Christianity and other

religions altogether, and so as to bring Britain into line with other countries.

This is the official position of the Church of England, the Roman Catholics, the Orthodox Jews, the militant Muslims, and some other religious organisations, of several Labour and other progressive politicians — and of 36 per cent of the population (according to the same survey). The obvious advantage is that the law would no longer discriminate between religions; the obvious disadvantages are that it would still discriminate between religion and other forms of belief, that it would probably remain uncertain, and that it would dramatically increase the power of fanatics to impose their views on the majority and to have them protected from criticism.

There would be serious questions of definition under such a law. Would it cover only 'major' religions, and if so which denominations and how would they be chosen and listed? Would it cover only monotheistic religions, and if so exclude Hindus and Buddhists? Would it cover all theistic religions, and would these be the several hundred denominations whose places of worship have been certified by the Registrar General, and if so include many highly objectionable organisations (such as Mormons and Moonies)? Would it cover all kinds of religion, and if so include even more questionable organisations (such as Spiritualists and Scientologists)? Would it cover non-religious beliefs and organisations — and if not, why not?

Commentators have sometimes proposed models for reform in the European and Indian laws against insulting any religion, but these aren't really very helpful. The former have proved to be unsatisfactory, since they are either oppressive or ineffective, and there is no reason to confine such protection to religion; the latter originally applied only to direct insults in the sight or hearing of believers, and again there is no reason to confine such protection to religion.

Restriction

A less easy but more obvious thing to do with the law would be to narrow it, by introducing into the definition of blasphemy the elements of an attack on religion, of an intent to make such an attack, and of a genuine tendency to a breach of the peace, and also by preventing private prosecutions, allowing the defence of public good, and admitting expert evidence (as in the Obscene Publications Acts). In a thorough reform such restrictions could be combined with the extension of the law to cover other or all religions. The advantage is that this would make the law clear and comprehensible; the disadvantage (for some people) is that it would make prosecutions very unlikely and convictions almost impossible.

This is the position of the minority of the Law Commission, of some Liberal and Reform Jews and progressive Christians, and many liberal-minded people (it wasn't offered in the survey). It follows what seems to be a good general principle that objectionable forms of speech and behaviour should be regulated by the law, which led to the relevant sections of the Race Relations Acts and may lead to additions to the Sexual Discrimination Act; but the experience of these laws is hardly encouraging. A similar change could be made by abolishing the present blasphemy law and replacing it with the addition of 'religious' to the 'racial' groups (defined 'by reference to colour, race, nationality or ethnic or national origins') which are protected from incitement to hatred by the Race Relations provisions of the Public Order Act. In Northern Ireland, indeed, the Prevention of Incitement to Hatred Act (Northern Ireland) of 1970 does protect 'religious belief' as well as 'custom, race or ethnic or national origins' from incitement to hatred; but this hardly seems to have had much useful effect in that area during the past two decades.

Abolition

In the end, however, the most desirable single thing to do with the common law of blasphemy is surely to abolish it (together with the obsolete ecclesiastical laws against heresy, schism and atheism) without replacing it with any new law. If there is a need to regulate offensive material about religion, to prevent either public disorder or private damage, this should be covered by the general law covering such areas, so that religious feelings or organisations have the same status as political feelings or organisations, and that religious topics have the same place as all other controversial subjects.

This is the position of the majority of the Law Commission, of the Humanist movement, of most of the civil liberties organisations, of several Labour and other progressive politicians, of most people in the fields of art and literature — and of 35 per cent of the population (according to the same survey). It has the great advantages of rationality and simplicity. The disadvantages are that it might be seen as a gratuitous blow at religion and a formal sign that nothing is held sacred in our society; but this sort of moralistic attitude is surely out of place in the sort of pluralist society ours has become.

★ ★ ★

Both sides in the controversy have appealed to the *European Convention on Human Rights* (1953), which puts into force much of the *Universal Declaration of Human Rights* (1948) and has been ratified by Great Britain. The relevant passages are Articles 9 and 10 (which follow Articles 18 and 19 of the *Universal Declaration*):

Article 9

1. Everyone has the right to freedom of thought, conscience and religion; this right includes freedom to change his religion or belief, and freedom, either alone or in community with others and in public or private, to manifest his religion or belief, in worship, teaching, practice and observance.

2. Freedom to manifest one's religion or beliefs shall be subject only to such limitations as are prescribed by law and are necessary in a democratic society in the interests of public safety, for the protection of public order, health or morals, or for the protection of the rights and freedoms of others.

Article 10

1. Everyone has the right to freedom of expression. This right shall include freedom to hold opinions and to receive and impart information and ideas without interference by public authority and regardless of frontiers. This Article shall not prevent States from requiring the licensing of broadcasting, television or cinema enterprises.

2. The exercise of these freedoms, since it carries with it duties and responsibilities, may be subject to such formalities, conditions, restrictions or penalties as are prescribed by law and are necessary in a democratic society, in the interests of national security, territorial integrity or public safety, for the prevention of disorder or crime, for the protection of health or morals, for the protection of the reputation or rights of others, for preventing the disclosure of information received in confidence, or for maintaining the authority and impartiality of the judiciary.

There is also an important addition in Article 14:

Article 14

The enjoyment of the rights and freedoms set forth in this convention shall be secured without discrimination on any ground such as sex, race, colour, language, religion, political or other opinion, national or social origin, association with a national minority, property, birth or other status.

These articles are vague enough to give plenty of room for argument on both sides. In the *Gay News* case, for example, on one side the editor and publisher of the poem argued that they had suffered discrimination on the grounds that the blasphemy law covers only Anglican Christianity and that the poem was prosecuted for its sexual orientation; while on the other side Scarman argued in the House of Lords that Article 9 'by necessary implication ... imposes a duty on all of us to refrain from insulting or outraging the religious feelings of others'. The European Commission explicitly rejected the *Gay News* argument in 1982 when it refused its appeal; and it implicitly rejected Scarman's argument in 1980 when it refused an application by the Scientologists against criticism in a Swedish newspaper and denied that freedom of religion includes freedom from criticism. Indeed the only necessary implication of Article 9 is surely that any insult or outrage must not interfere with freedom of thought, conscience, or religion, as well as not causing a breach of the peace. After all, the *European Convention* also provides for freedom of political, social, and sexual activity, but this does not impose the duty to refrain from insulting or outraging the political, social, or sexual feelings of others! In fact a moment's thought will show that mere offence — feeling insulted or outraged — should not be the basis of restriction of freedom of expression, since it would lead to the suppression of all controversial discussion of any subject.

The situation would hardly be improved by extending the blasphemy law to cover all religions, since this would only replace discrimination in favour of one particular religion by discrimination in favour of religion in general. As is recognised in the *European Convention* itself, there are other forms of belief which are not religious but are just as strongly held. Scarman argued that, 'in an increasingly plural society such as that of modern Britain, it is necessary not only to respect the differing religious beliefs, feelings and practices of all, but also to protect them from scurrility, vilification, ridicule, and contempt'. But this line of interpretation would make it illegal to insult or outrage any strong feelings of any kind held by anyone, which would be a formula not for a plural society but for a closed society in which no one could say anything offensive about anything. After all, everything offends someone and everyone is offended by something. The most rational course would be to abolish all laws discriminating either in favour of or against any kind of feeling and to recognise that the only limits to freedom of expression in a more or less open society should be whether it intentionally or recklessly causes public disorder or private damage.

14 Conclusion

Blasphemy is bound to exist wherever religion exists, in the sense that any unfavourable comment on a religion tends to offend its followers and may lead to a breach of the peace. But blasphemy isn't bound to be punished as a criminal offence — indeed punishing the blasphemer only makes matters worse, since it never suppresses the blasphemy and it always increases the offence on both sides. The blasphemy law has survived as a relic of religious persecution in our society for three centuries, but it has never done any good either to religion or to society or to the blasphemers. It has been condemned by Freethinkers for more than two centuries, and it has been criticised by many other people for more than a century.

Perhaps the most powerful attack came from James Fitzjames Stephen, writing after the *Freethinker* case in 1884. He argued against the distinction between the matter and the manner of material accused of blasphemy:

You cannot really distinguish between substance and style. You must either forbid or permit all attacks on Christianity .... You cannot in practice send a man to gaol for not writing like a scholar and a gentleman when he is neither one nor the other, and when he is writing on a subject which excites him strongly.

He warned against the danger of extending the law to cover all religions, and he raised the position of unbelievers:

If the law were really impartial and punished blasphemy only because it offends the feelings of believers, it ought also to punish such preaching as offends the feelings of unbelievers. All the more earnest and enthusiastic forms of religion are extremely offensive to those who do not believe them.

He concluded that the best course would be to abolish the law altogether:

Such an abolition would not only secure complete liberty of opinion on these matters, but it would prevent the recurrence at irregular intervals of scandalous prosecutions, which have never in any one instance benefited any one, least of all the cause which they were intended to serve, and which sometimes afford a channel for the gratification of private malice under the cloak of religion.

Hypatia Bradlaugh Bonner, writing during the last wave of prosecutions of Freethought propagandists, said in *Penalties Upon Opinion* (1912) that religious persecution 'has sometimes killed the heretic, but it has never killed the heresy', and added that in the latest treatment of blasphemy 'this persecution is reduced to its most contemptible, most futile form'.

J. B. Bury, writing at the same time, said in his *History of Freedom of Thought* (1913) that the blasphemy law embodied little more than class distinctions:

The present administration of the common law in regard to blasphemy does not endanger the liberty of those unbelievers who have the capacity for contributing to progress. But it violates the supreme principle of liberty of opinion and discussion. It hinders uneducated people from saying in the only ways in which they know how to say it, what those who have been brought up differently say, with impunity, far more effectively and far more insidiously .... Thus the law, as now administered, simply penalises bad taste and places disabilities upon uneducated freethinkers.

What has changed since then, curiously enough, is that attempts have been made to use the law not so much against crude attacks on religion as against more sophisticated comments on religion — against the broadcasters of serious drama or comic serials, against minority magazines publishing serious poems, against serious producers of classic plays, against serious makers of minority videos, against reputable publishers of serious novels, and so on. This hardly makes the law any better; instead it makes it not only oppressive but ridiculous.

'The law is a dreary thing,' as D. H. Lawrence said when he came up against it in 1929, 'and its judgements have nothing to do with life.' But it is there, and has to be taken into account. There is a serious argument for a law against direct attacks on religion (or any other controversial subject) in public places or in the sight or hearing of believers of a kind which might cause a breach of the peace; but there are already adequate if not excessive laws in this area. There is no serious argument for a law against attacks on religion in private places or in publications, when such attacks are witnessed only through voluntary action; and this is what the blasphemy law is. It is needed by habitual offendees who seek out offence (especially by those people who are offended that other people are not offended by what they find offensive), and not by innocent victims of gratuitous attack. No Christians have to read Voltaire or Paine or the *Freethinker* or *Gay News* or see *Monty Python's Life of Brian* or *Visions of Ecstasy,* and no Muslims have to read Dante or Voltaire or *The Satanic Verses,* just as no unbelievers have to read what are to them the equally offensive Bible (Old or New Testament) or *Koran.* It is long past time for this last relic of religious persecution to be abolished, and for religion — like all other forms of belief and behaviour — to stand or fall without special protection in an open society.

This condemnation of legal protection for religious feelings is intended as a condemnation not so much of religious feelings themselves as of legal protection for any feelings, however sensitive or sacred. Religious liberty (like political liberty) involves freedom from as well as freedom for religion, and includes the freedom to reject or attack as well as to adopt or defend any religious (or other) belief or behaviour. In a more or less free society, everyone and everything must be open to question and criticism, however unpleasant or unfair, so that we may hear every side of every case and make up our own minds in the light of both reason and emotion. Such freedom is dangerous, of course, but its absence is more dangerous. Free thought and free speech may make trouble, but attempts to suppress them make worse trouble. More harm is caused by the persecution than by the practice of any objectionable form of expression, including blasphemy.

The final consideration is that perhaps we should listen to our children when they chant the traditional answer to insult:

> Sticks and stones may break my bones,
> But words can never hurt me!

It is time to answer words with words, not with the sticks and stones of the blasphemy law.

Further Reading

The following list gives only some of the many relevant books in English (including classics which are outdated but still valuable), and none of the many more pamphlets and articles. The best sources of information about the practice and punishment of blasphemy are the original publications and records; the main cases in Britain are included in the standard Law Reports, and several were reported in Freethought periodicals and often in separate publications.

Religious Persecution & Toleration

Edward Gibbon *The Decline and Fall of the Roman Empire* (1776-1788), H. T. Buckle *Introduction to the History of Civilization* (1856-1861, 1904), W. E. H. Lecky *History of the Rise and Influence of the Spirit of Rationalism in Europe* (1865) and *History of European Morals from Augustus to Charlemagne* (1869), H. C. Lea *A History of the Inquisition* (1888-1908, 1922), E. S. P. Haynes *Religious Persecution* (1904), Francesco Ruffini *Religious Liberty* (1912), J. B. Bury *A History of Freedom of Thought* (1913, 1952), W. K. Jordan *The Development of Religious Toleration in England* (1932-1940), Joseph Lecler *Tolerance and the Reformation* (1960), Henry Kamen *The Rise of Toleration* (1967), Leonard W. Levy *Treason Against God* (1981).

Heresy & Blasphemy Law

William Stubbs *The Constitutional History of England in Its Origin and Development* Volume 3 (1878), James Fitzjames Stephen *A History of the English Criminal Law* Volume 2 (1883), William Holdsworth *A History of English Law* Volume 8 (1925), G. D. Nokes *A History of the Crime of Blasphemy* (1928), St John A. Robilliard *Religion and the Law* (1984).

Censorship

Hypatia Bradlaugh Bonner *Penalties Upon Opinion* (1912, 1913, 1934), W. H. Wickwar *The Struggle for the Freedom of the Press* (1928), Donald Thomas *A Long Time Burning* (1969), Arthur Calder-Marshall *Lewd, Blasphemous and Obscene* (1972), Paul O'Higgins *Censorship in Britain* (1972), David Tribe *Questions of Censorship* (1973), Edward J. Bristow *Vice and Vigilance* (1977).

Freethought

J. M. Robertson *A Short History of Freethought* (1899, 1906, 1915, 1936) and *A History of Freethought in the Nineteenth Century* (1929), David Tribe *100 Years of Freethought* (1967), Edward Royle *Victorian Infidels* (1974) and *Radicals, Secularists and Republicans* (1980), Jim Herrick *Vision and Realism* (1982) and *Against the Faith* (1985).